A Likely Story

A Likely Story

Probability and Play in Fiction

Robert Newsom

Rutgers University Press
New Brunswick and London

Library of Congress Cataloging-in-Publication Data

Newsom, Robert, 1944–
 A likely story.

 Includes bibliographies and index.
  1. Fiction—History and criticism. 2.Probabilities
in literature. 3. Literature—Philosophy. I. Title.
PN3347.N48 1988   809.3'91   87-38128
ISBN 0-8135-1320-O
ISBN 0-8135-1357-X (pbk.)

British Cataloging-in-Publication information available

In Memoriam

Julia Valentine Winslow Newsom

Ewart Walker Newsom

Contents

Acknowledgments

I am grateful to several people who gave me help of various kinds, including putting me onto useful sources, sharing their own work before its publication, offering counterarguments, and reading and commenting on drafts of the whole. I want especially to thank Robert L. Caserio and Peter Lamarque (who served as readers for the publisher), Homer O. Brown, Alexander Gelley, Robert L. Montgomery, Jane O. Newman, Geoffrey Nunberg, Douglas Lane Patey, Hilary Schor, Martin Schwab, and Deanna Wilkes-Gibbs. I am also very grateful to my students at Irvine in Criticism 100B who cheerfully rode my hobbyhorse with me over the often difficult terrain of probability.

But in this, as in all things, my deepest debts have been to my family—Linda, Catherine, and Andy.

A Likely Story

Introduction

Probability is generally understood by philosophers as the concept we use when we seek or describe factual knowledge of things about which we have incomplete knowledge—in other words, when we want to know something about the world but can't find incontrovertible evidence about it. Where we cannot have certain knowledge, our knowledge must be probable at best. Probability as an instrument of judgment helps us toward knowledge in the face of uncertainty (that is, even—or especially—when we cannot hope to resolve *all* doubts), and the sort of knowledge that probability helps us toward is therefore said to be probable or to have probability or sometimes even to *be* a probability.

Probability also has throughout most of the history of literary theory been a concept thought to provide a standard against which to judge literary works, as when Aristotle tells us that a tragedy's plot ought to represent actions that conform to necessity or probability.

This study deals with the history of ideas about probability both as they have been applied to literary fictions and to questions about the real world. It is especially interested in the relations between philosophical and literary concepts of probability. It is therefore about the logical relations between the fictional and the real, and so it is most fundamentally about the very nature of fiction itself.

For most of the history of literary theory, from Aristotle down through the end of the eighteenth century at least, a logic or standard of probability has been an essential feature of accounts of literary judgment and interpretation, but generally these accounts do not question the logical ground of literary probability, and it is often the case that critics simply assume their readers know what is meant by probability or repeat variants of definitions that have been traditional since Plato and Aristotle. It is no longer the case that critics centrally appeal to probabilistic standards, partly because it has come to be widely assumed that appeals to probability entail a naïve realism. There is indeed a serious problem with applying a probabilistic logic to fictions, but there is too an equally naïve antirealism entailed in the belief that probabilistic fictional logics can be effectively escaped or transcended. Even though the heyday of literary probability has long passed, we all continue to understand (and at least occasionally and informally to make) such statements as, "The character of Kurtz is certainly exceptional, but nonetheless probable given the circumstances," or, "The plot of *Oliver Twist* is too full of coincidences to be probable," or, "It is not unlikely that Tess would have a red ribbon in her hair."

The importance of probability as a concept necessary to our understanding of the *real* world can hardly be overemphasized. Because we must invoke a probabilistic logic whenever we do not have certain knowledge about something we want to know, and because in a skeptical age it is considered impossible to have certain knowledge about any matters of actual fact, it has come to be recognized by philosophers that we must have recourse to probabilities whenever we have questions about facts in the real world. The point is not of simply philosophical significance. It is literally the case that virtually all modern science outside the purely abstract branches of mathematics could not exist without highly developed instruments of probabilistic inference. And in such basic areas as physics, genetics, and information theory, probabilistic functions have come increasingly to be recognized as absolutely foundational. Indeed, modern information theory became possible only when information itself was for the first time actually *defined* probabilistically, as that which reduces uncertainty.[1]

Interestingly, it is only relatively recently that philosophers have begun to worry much about what is meant by *probability*. Typically throughout most of its philosophical history as well as its literary history, it has been used without definition or with only a cursory attempt at definition, and definitions have often appeared inconsistent, even within single writers. Plato defines the probable as what the vulgar mob believe. Aristotle defines the probable as what the wise believe *and* as what usually happens. These seem to be quite different things, for if we share Plato's feelings about the mob, we will no doubt think that what the wise believe and what the vulgar mob believe are different things. Moreover, what the wise believe and what usually happens seem to be quite different things because what the wise believe plainly refers to a subjective thing, a property of people's minds, while what usually happens refers to an objective thing, a property of the world out there. It makes sense for me to say I believe in Napoleon's existence because that is what most people believe, and it makes sense for me to say I believe I will probably live to seventy-one because that is how long people of my actuarial set do usually (on the average) live. But it doesn't make sense for me to say that I believe in Napoleon's existence because that is what usually happens or that I believe I will live to seventy-one because that is what most people believe. So perhaps when we speak about probability we are speaking not about one concept but many.

And yet it is not hard to see a fundamental unity among these different senses of the probable. Presumably the wise believe much of what they believe based upon their experience of what usually happens (as well as upon the testimony of *other* wise people who also base beliefs upon their experience of what usually happens—as well as upon the testimony of *other* wise people, and so on and so on; in other words, accepting the testimony of people on the way to probable knowledge is simply a way of enlarging one's experience of what usually happens). Thus it is not hard to work a sense of what usually happens into statements about my belief in Napoleon's existence. I can say I believe in Napoleon's existence because it usually happens that historians believe in it. Similarly, I can say that I believe the chances are I will live to seventy-one because, based upon their experience of what usually happens, that is what statistical experts believe. That there are uncomfortable entanglements of the subjective and objective here may be unfortunate, but it does not mean that there are fundamentally different kinds of probability. (In fact, this difficulty over subject and object still vexes modern theories of probability.)

It seems harder to make Plato's sense of the probable as what the mob believe consistent with these definitions, but even this proves to be not difficult when we consider that, except under very controlled or very noncontroversial conditions, people will tend to disagree about what actually is probable or not or about *how* probable a certain thing may be. Plato's definition of the probable as what the mob believe can be understood as distancing Plato's beliefs from vulgar opinion and devaluing knowledge that is not certain rather than as introducing a fundamentally or logically novel concept of probability. What the mob believe is based upon their (defective) sense of what usually happens; we—the wiser—know better, but if we're Platonists, we may not be much interested in knowledge that falls short of certainty. The vulgar are content with probabilities; the wise seek certainty.

Some philosophers and intellectual historians would argue for radically different senses of probability. Expositors of the mathematical theory of probability will often say things like, "Of course, we aren't concerned with probability in the ordinary sense." And the most important recent historian of probability has argued that around 1660 there is a fundamentally new concept of probability born, one that makes the mathematical theory possible. Other historians see a fundamental continuity in the history of probability, but nevertheless talk about "shifts of meaning," as though at certain moments the concept as a whole came to mean something different.

I shall instead here assume and elsewhere argue in greater detail that there has been at least since Aristotle a concept of probability whose fundamental shape has remained more or less constant. This concept presents a series of aspects—sometimes offered as definitions of the concept as a whole—that throughout its history have proven difficult to keep apart even though some aspects at times seem inconsistent —such as the subjective and objective aspects just mentioned. The fact that all these aspects seem to seek one another out suggests that at root they really all do belong to the same concept. This is by no means to deny historical change, nor is it to say that whenever we encounter the word *probability* we may be confident about what is intended, for particular writers usually are referring only to limited aspects of probability. And it is certainly not the case that the aspects of probability are always consistent with one another, much less the same. It is the rule in the history of probability that writers have tended not to appreciate the whole shape of the concept, and thus an enormous amount of confusion and controversy has been generated.

There are signs that the concept of probability is coming to be recognized as among the central and inescapable topics for intellectual history. A dozen years ago, the philosopher Ian Hacking published a short book called *The Emergence of Probability* that was partially inspired by some remarks of Michel Foucault in *The Order of Things*, but also more generally inspired by the application of Foucault's historical method to Hacking's earlier interest in the logic of probability.[2] Hacking's book tries to answer a very specific historical question: Why is it that calculations about probabilities suddenly spring up in a wide variety of places all at the same time—around the year 1660—when the actual mathematics required in such calculations was extremely simple and had long been available? Hacking's answer to his question, most briefly put, is that before 1660 there in fact simply didn't exist the modern concept of probability, and in order to show that, Hacking has to say a great deal about just what is meant by *probability*. In the process of coming up with that answer, Hacking tells a fascinating story that succeeds in showing how far-reaching are the implications of probabilistic thinking and how central is the concept of probability to all the great problems of modern thought—problems concerning language, rationality, the limits of knowledge, and the like. It perhaps testifies most strongly—if ironically—to the success of his book that the Hacking thesis, as it has come to be called, continues to engage the imaginations of scholars in a wide range of disciplines even though the thesis has in important respects been shown to be wrong. That is, while Hacking's claim that certain sorts of probabilistic propositions simply aren't possible before 1660 has been shown to be mistaken (and he himself admits its exaggerations and simplifications),[3] nevertheless scholars are coming to recognize as very significant his observation that the mystery to be answered is not only why the mathematics of probability should be born suddenly at several places all at the same time, but why probabilities of every sort are at that same time suddenly, as he puts it, "on every pen."[4] Thanks to Hacking's book as well as such more recent accounts as Barbara Shapiro's *Probability and Certainty in Seventeenth-Century England* (subtitled "A Study of the Relationships between Natural Science, Religion, History, Law, and Literature"), what used to look like an age of certainty now looks much more like an age of the merely probable, if not an age of downright doubt.[5]

This relatively recent interest among intellectual historians in the concept of probability has fortunately begun to find its way into literary studies. The first third of Paula Backscheider's 1979 collection called *Probability, Time, and Space in Eighteenth-Century Literature* contains valuable essays by Margaret J. Osler, Paul K. Alkon, Paul J. Korshin, and Hoyt Trowbridge.[6] More recent is Douglas Lane Patey's excellent and enormously learned study, *Probability and Literary Form: Philosophic Theory and Literary Practice in the Augustan Age.*[7]

Important as the intellectual history of the changing aspects of the concept of probability is to our purposes, however, I should emphasize that the present study's interest in that history is in a sense secondary in that our need to explore it is generated by a more basic question, one that emerges when we ask what is the relationship between literary and other sorts of probability. Looking for that relationship, we shall see that there is a fundamental logical oddity entailed whenever we invoke probabilities in connection with fictions. As has already been suggested, the whole point of probabilistic logic is to help us when we do not have certain knowledge about some question—when we are in other words uncertain or in doubt. But literary fictions do not raise real doubts. We *know* that there never was any Kurtz or Oliver Twist or Tess. Indeed, we are more certain about our knowledge of such fictional beings than we can ever be about real persons. The evidence I might have concerning Napoleon, for example, is effectively infinite, but what I can know about Oliver is neatly limited to the evidence of the text of the book in which he appears. It is all there, and there is nothing to be doubted. Asserting that "The plot of *Oliver Twist* is too full of coincidences to be probable" is logically not only unnecessary, but nonsensical. Either I enter the fictional world, so to speak, and accept the pretense of the fiction, accept the "facts" of the plot as they are presented to me, or I remain in the real world, so to speak, and recognize the "facts" of the novel as plainly fictional—that is, "false." In either case, there ought to be no question of ascribing degrees of probability to the novel's plot, for from the standpoint of the world of fiction the events it describes do not put us in doubt because they are certainly true, while from the standpoint of the real world they do not put us in doubt because they are certainly false.

Because the logical oddity involved in ascribing probability to fiction has not to my knowledge been recognized as such before now (it differs in several important respects from the claim that invoking literary probability entails a naïve realism), and since it will be convenient to refer to it frequently, I shall give it a name. I shall call this oddity the antinomy of fictional probability. That it hasn't been recognized before now may suggest several things, not the least of which is that it is itself unreal—that it only *appears* to present us with a logical problem. There are, indeed would have to be, many ways around the antinomy, or it would by now be ancient history. Our questions are, therefore, to what extent are those ways logical ones—if they prove logical, the antinomy isn't real—and, if they don't prove logical, how is it that they have so successfully kept the antinomy hidden? What, if anything, is it that justifies all the literary judgments from Aristotle on that invoke some sort of probabilistic standard?

The answers to these questions clearly have to do with the very nature of fiction itself. And fictionality is as large, important, and controversial a topic as probability, within literary studies and without. If probabilistic judgments have been central to literary criticism for much of its history, they have been so precisely as an important means of justifying or at least lending respectability to literature in the face of an ancient and persistent embarrassment: that it deals in things manifestly untrue. A narrative may be obviously false, and yet if it can be said to have probability it has nonetheless been brought at least into some apparently acceptable relation with the true. If the worry about literature's fictionality has substantially lessened, curiosity about its nature certainly has increased, along with the conviction that fictionality is far more prevalent and necessary to our mental lives than was formerly thought. Theories of fiction abound in contemporary philosophy and especially in what has come to be known as cognitive science.[8]

But while the significance of fictionality as a topic of modern inquiry may be as apparent as that of probability, there is no more agreement about the nature of fiction than about probability. So in asking the question, What does it mean to ascribe probability to a fiction? we have to explore in some detail both the nature of probability and the nature of fiction. In my view they are in fact very closely related, even interdependent, and some accounts of probability turn out to be uncannily like some accounts of fiction.

The argument of this study is I think not very difficult, at least not technically so, in spite of the fact that the theory of probability and the theory of fiction can themselves both be extremely difficult and technical. Ironically, the most difficult aspect of this study may for many readers be to keep in mind that there is a problem about ascribing probability to fictions at all. This is because even among people without special literary interests, entertaining fictions is so much second nature—indeed, it may be first nature, an essentially human faculty —that such probabilistic statements as those I have used about Kurtz, Oliver, and Tess seem, and in some sense are, transparently comprehensible. We are much more likely simply to jump into the discussion and assent or take exception to the particular probabilistic judgment than to question its underlying logic. So there may be difficulties enough to justify an overview of the argument here, and for clarity's sake I shall state my conclusions first.

Both the antinomy of fictional probability and the ways we have of working around it (and indeed of ignoring it) arise from what is in my view the most important feature of fictions, that in imaginatively entertaining them we necessarily split ourselves between real and fictional worlds. Such a split, I argue, is invisible to the game of entertaining fictions, for to recognize the split is to end the game. And the game is a good deal more difficult to get out of than is often supposed. For although critics, theorists, and philosophers routinely think of themselves as existing outside the game, practically speaking this turns out to be an impossible point of view to sustain. Thus something like a "scientific" theory of literature in which the theorist stands outside the game understanding it from some higher metalevel is an impossibility, and the literary theory of fiction turns out to be something one has to do *within* fiction.

Probabilistic talk about fictions is peculiarly interesting because while it does not really render the split within players visible, it does accommodate it and might be said even to negotiate it in important ways. Talk about literary probabilities is talk about the relation between real and fictional worlds, which is much more to the point than talk simply about the nature of one sort of world or the other. For whatever else is true of real and fictional worlds, it is only in examining the relations between them that we can hope to come to an understanding of their natures. Indeed, they don't have natures, we might say, independent of those relations. While there is, strictly speaking, no logical way to engage in probabilistic talk about fictions (without, that is, violating either logic on the one hand or the integrity of the fiction on the other), such talk nonetheless is peculiarly useful in letting the game of fiction go on, and, in particular, in letting it go on in some public and communal fashion—not just within individual readers, but among an audience as the game called criticism. Probabilistic talk about fictions provides a way for players to compare games or even conjoin private games into larger public ones. It is on this account that ascribing probability to fiction has proven, in spite of the logical and theoretical problems it poses, so useful to criticism.

Although literary probability has rather sober connotations (*probability* is cognate with *probation* and *probity*), one of our conclusions will be that talk about literary probabilities in fact points toward the essentially playful nature of fiction and specifically to the activity of make-believe. Talk about probability is no less useful for negotiating the related distinction between the "serious" and the "nonserious" than it is useful for negotiating the distinction between "fact" and "fiction." In the last part of this study we will try to see how the account developed concerning fiction also helps us to understand some important features of the origins of the novel and the role played in those origins by such oppositions as, in addition to the "serious" and "nonserious," the "childish" and the "grown-up," an opposition I believe to have been peculiarly important for the history of the English novel especially.

There are a number of things that need to be established on the way to these conclusions. I have already suggested one of the most important of these: that there is a fundamental unity shared by concepts of probability from Aristotle through the present; for without such unity the antinomy would appear to be circumvented. As has already been indicated, it is by no means uncontroversial to claim for concepts of probability a fundamental unity, however. Many who have contributed to ideas about probability fairly recently have in fact assumed that the word is essentially equivocal and that there is one kind of probability we make use of when we make statistical calculations in connection with some random phenomenon and quite another we make use of when we make guesses about more complex happenings in the face of very incomplete knowledge. Even if it develops that the statistician's probability is at the deepest logical level the same as, say, the historian's, it needs further to be established that both the statistician's (or, more generally, scientist's) probability and the historian's are fundamentally the same as the literary critic's. And it needs further to be established that what Ian Hacking has called the logical space of probability, that is its most basic logical purpose or function, has not substantially changed since Aristotle's day. Hacking, as we have seen, argues that it is precisely the logical space occupied by our modern concept that doesn't itself exist until around the latter part of the seventeenth century. I take issue with that view, though I shall by no means claim that particular criteria of probability have not substantially evolved—or, perhaps more accurately, revolved—since Aristotle, nor most particularly that the kinds of evidence implied by those criteria have not substantially changed. But it is one thing for the rules of a logic to change (as when one sort of evidence comes to be valued over others); it is quite another for the fundamental function of the logic itself to change. I hope to show that the logical space occupied by probability remains very much the same for us as it was for Aristotle.

It is with Aristotle that the argument begins. Looking at the definitions Aristotle offers of probability in the *Poetics* and the *Rhetoric* among other places, and distinguishing them from Plato's rather less interesting and less useful definition, we shall in the first part discover a number of interconnected associations within probability that cling to the concept throughout its history. Already in Aristotle's concept there is a serious problem unremarked by Aristotle himself that looks forward to the modern problematics both of probability theory (what after Hume's discussion of it has come to be known as the problem of induction) and of fictional theory. We shall then trace some main lines of the subsequent history of philosophical thinking about probability up into the twentieth century to look at the two large questions already sketched: the question of whether there has been a fundamentally new logical space opened up for the modern concept of probability and the question of whether our modern concept is deeply equivocal or not. The negative answers both questions will receive will validate our looking for some fundamental unity in the history of literary thinking about probability as well as our seeing some fundamental unity between literary and other sorts of probability.

Basing itself upon these findings, part two will focus more exclusively upon the history of ideas about probability among literary theorists, chiefly in the Renaissance with its reclamation of Aristotle and through the period that sees the beginnings and rise of the novel. It is in this span that the most dramatic event in the history of probability occurs—the birth of mathematical probability—and we shall see that the events accompanying that birth have close parallels in the no less dramatic birth of the novel. Moreover, in this period literary discussions of probability are pushed sufficiently far so as to bring them to the very brink of discovering what I have called the antinomy of literary probability.

Part three will be concerned with establishing a theory of fictional probability that accounts for the antinomy—without exactly doing away with it. Central to this enterprise is the question of the sort of belief one may be said to entertain about fictions. Probability always concerns belief (some philosophers claim that any probabilistic assertion is necessarily an assertion about one's beliefs), and literary probability can often not only be closely connected to, but actually identified with, credibility. Asking questions about the nature of our belief in fictions will in turn lead us to question the nature of pretending, and pretending is the activity that finally explains the antinomy of fictional probability.

The conclusion looks both forward and back. We shall discuss what some of the practical consequences of our conclusions might be after our account of fictions as instruments of pretending has first led us to examine some questions about play and to return to historical considerations concerning the rise of the novel. I shall argue for deep connections among the histories of the concepts of probability, fiction, and the grown-up and suggest some ways in which those interconnections might lead us to revise our account of the origins of the novel.

Having offered this overview of the scope and argument of this study, I should perhaps emphasize one thing that it emphatically is *not* about except incidentally: it makes no attempt to look comprehensively at ways in which probability has been *thematized* in fiction—that is, the ways in which fictions have themselves conceptualized probability or employed probabilistic logics for their own ends. Such would, I think, be a very interesting study in its own right and would certainly have a bearing on our own historical account of the origins of the novel and how those origins are connected to changing ideas about probability in philosophy and science developing contemporaneously with the rise of fiction. There are two reasons for this exclusion. The first is that a history of the thematization of probability in fiction would be a vast undertaking. The second is that such a study begs the very question upon which I want to focus, which is the way in which a literary *critical* probabilistic logic is used to negotiate the relation between the fictional and the real. To look at how a narrative thinks about doubt, expectation, chance, likelihood (or any of the vast array of ideas dependent upon probability) is to adopt the fiction's standpoint, which is to overlook the fact that we are in so doing ourselves entering a particular fictional world. It is of course entirely possible and usual within fictions to make nonfictional assertions, to say things about reality that are as true as the things one can say in any nonfictional discourse. True things can be said in a novel about the Battle of Waterloo or the characteristics of electrons. And thematizations of probability in fictions involve assertions of this kind. Paradoxically, therefore, thematizations of probability in fiction are themselves for the most part not fictional and therefore don't shed light upon the logic of fictions or of fictional probability.[9] Our job will be to keep in mind, therefore, that the question for us is not so much what the fiction thinks about probability, but what probability thinks and can tell us about the fiction.

Part One
The Philosophical Traditions

Chapter I

Aristotle

ARISTOTLE is the starting point for discussions of literary probability of course because he makes important and famous reference to the probable in several difficult passages of the *Poetics*. But he does not himself offer a definition of probability there. He refers to the concept as though we all knew perfectly well what it means, and perhaps this is why subsequent commentators tend not to question its meaning or at most to ask what kind of probability Aristotle had in mind rather than the more fundamental question of what he meant by the probable. Elsewhere, as we shall see, Aristotle does offer definitions of the probable, but while they are consistent with his references to the probable in the *Poetics*, they pose some serious difficulties — difficulties that turn out to be prophetic, for they look forward to various controversies that have surrounded probability throughout its history and that remain controversial today. In this section we shall examine some of those difficulties.

In English, the concept of the probable bears the stamp of its Latin derivation from *probabilis,* meaning the provable and the *a*pprovable, which in turn derives from the verb *probare,* meaning to test (*probe* is a modern derivative) or approve. That in turn comes from *probus,* meaning simply virtuous or good (and giving us the modern *probity*). Many of the English cognates are not only judicious in their connotations but positively judicial: in addition to *probe* and *probity* there are *probation* and *probate.* But it is also the institution of logic as well as the law that is represented in such other English cognates as *proof* and *prove.* There are as well modern derivatives that more directly convey the connection in Latin with virtue in *probus: improve, reprove,* and *reprobate.*

Aristotle's somewhat obscure but extremely influential concept of the probable also implies something approvable, at least—if not something positively virtuous—but his usual word for it has a very different root meaning than the Latin. Sometimes an English translator will rendor *endoxon* (general opinion) as "probability,"[1] and we shall understand why this is so presently; but the word of Aristotle's that is most often translated as the "probable" is *to eikos,* which derives from *eikon,* meaning image or likeness and giving us *icon* (and very little else except the prefix *icono-*). Thus a closer translation for Aristotle's word (were it not for the desirability of emphasizing the continuity of the subsequent history of the concept especially through medieval Latin and into French and then English) would be the "likely," which in fact retains much of the meaning of *to eikos* lost in the "probable." Indeed, Aristotle's terminology suggests as a closer Latin equivalent *verisimilis,* the "verisimilar," which the Romans took to be the literal translation of *to eikos.* Verisimilitude, we shall see, is a concept that is impossible to detach from probability, though the attempt has often been made. (In fact in German today the one word that renders *probability* is the *wahrscheinlich,* a literal German rendering of verisimilar, for which it is also the unique translation, so that in German one can distinguish between probability and verisimilitude only with qualifiers.) A standard classical English-Greek dictionary (Liddell and Scott) interprets the likeness of *to eikos* as "like truth," and there is warrant for this in Plato's definition of the probable in the *Phaedrus* as possessed of a "likeness to truth," although, as one might expect, for Plato the likeness is more often than not illusory, and it is out of this sense that we derive a sense of *verisimilitude* as a merely illusory appearance of the truth. For the rhetorician, the probable is nothing other "than that which commends itself to the multitude," and what the multitude believes will be appealed to by the skillful speaker before the truth is, so that "even actual facts ought sometimes not be stated, if they don't tally with probability; . . . whatever you say, you simply must pursue this probability they talk of, and can say good-bye to the truth forever" (272e–273b; 273d).[2]

Aristotle's fullest discussions and definitions of the probable come in the *Prior Analytics* and the *Art of Rhetoric.* There, probabilities are taken to be, along with signs, the material out of which are built arguments which are analogous to the syllogisms employed in dialectics, though they lack certainty. These arguments, which Aristotle calls enthymemes, are common in rhetoric, which of course concerns itself only with matters that are open to dispute, subject to judgment, and therefore by their very nature not certain. (Aristotle's enthymemes should not be confused with those of the modern logician; today an enthymeme is defined rather differently and more narrowly as a syllogism that is missing one of its terms.) In the *Prior Analytics,* Aristotle defines a probability as "a generally approved proposition: what men know to happen or not to happen, to be or not to be, for the most part thus and thus, is a probability, e.g. 'the envious hate,' 'the beloved show affection'" (70a).[3] In the *Art of Rhetoric,* where the context is a discussion of the kinds of propositions a speaker will need to make use of in framing persuasive arguments, he says, "The Probable is that which usually happens; (with a limitation, however, which is sometimes forgotten—namely that the thing *may* happen otherwise:) the Probable being related to that in respect of which it is probable as Universal to Particular" (1357a–b).[4] That is to say, it is a proposition whose truth is not necessary but usual and which is related to whatever conclusion is to be arrived at as universals are related to particulars. As one commentator puts it, "an *eikos* is the major premiss in an argument of the form 'B as a rule is A, C is B, Therefore C is probably A,'"[5] although perhaps significantly in the examples Aristotle himself gives, there is no explicit qualification "as a rule" or "probably." He simply says, "the envious hate" and "the beloved show affection," as though the probability and the propositions were identical more than that probability were a qualification or an attribute attached to them.

In both texts, the definitions of the probable are accompanied by quite difficult discussions that attempt, not very successfully, to distinguish between probabilities and signs. In the *Rhetoric,* Aristotle asserts that probabilities and signs correspond to propositions that are respectively contingent and necessary, but immediately thereafter he distinguishes between signs that are themselves contingent (e.g., Socrates' wisdom and justice are together a contingent sign of the justice of all wise men) and those that are themselves necessary (e.g., lactation is a necessary sign in a woman of motherhood). It is not at all easy to see what, for Aristotle, distinguishes probabilities from contingent signs. In part it seems to be that all probabilities relate to the conclusions derived from them as universals relate to particulars, whereas contingent signs, we are told, may relate to their conclusions either as universals to particulars ("for instance, if one were to say that it is a sign that this man has a fever because he breathes hard") or as particulars to universals ("for instance, if one were to say that all wise men are just, because Socrates was both wise and just.") This difference will prove significant in the *Poetics,* but here the more important (and unspoken) difference seems rather to be that probabilities are propositions or premises, whereas signs are in themselves merely observations, and as such they can be only parts of propositions. Probabilities are sentences, whereas signs are nouns or noun clauses. Probabilities contain their own conclusions, but signs point to conclusions outside themselves. It is enough to say, "'The envious hate' is a probability," but never enough to say merely that "'the envious hate' is a sign." But clearly probabilities and contingent signs are closely related if not identical. If it is a probability that the envious hate, envy is a contingent sign of hatred. And signs may themselves lead to probabilities. The combination of wisdom and justice in Socrates, for example, may be a sign that points to the probability that all wise men are just.

It is not our task to resolve the difficulties of Aristotle's classifications, and for our purposes the confusion between probabilities and signs will itself prove informative enough because it suggests a relation between inductive evidence (signs) and probability that will be made explicit in the seventeenth century and that forms an essential part of modern probability theory. There is another difficulty or confusion in Aristotle's account that will prove equally significant. What seems so far to be clear are two fairly fundamental but important things: first, it follows from the importance of probability in building persuasive arguments that probability is for Aristotle an attribute of propositions that determines their credibility, or rather probabilities are propositions with high degrees of credibility; second, we have seen that probability may be an attribute of propositions either insofar as they have already been believed and testified to (as "generally approved proposition[s]") or insofar as experience tends to corroborate them (the probable being that which "usually [though not necessarily] happens"). But this second finding points to other difficult questions: What exactly is the source of a probable proposition's authority? Why should we believe a probability? How do we weigh the credibility of probabilities against other evidence? When Aristotle turns to more specific discussions about proofs, particularly when he discusses witnesses among the kinds of proof offered in courts of law, he helps us to frame these questions more precisely, even if he again provides no final answers to them.

According to Aristotle in the *Rhetoric,* there are two kinds of witnesses, the ancient and the recent, by which he means very roughly the celebrated dead on the one hand and on the other the celebrated living—in addition to those who share the risk of the trial. Probabilities come up in the context of the discussion of how one argues when there are *no* witnesses to speak for or against a point.

> In regard to the confirmation of evidence, when a man has no witnesses, he can say that the decision should be given in accordance with probabilities, and that this is the meaning of the oath "according to the best of one's judgement"; that probabilities cannot be bribed to deceive, and that they cannot be convicted of bearing false witness. [This incorruptibility has already been noted by Aristotle as a great advantage of the testimony of the dead.] But if a man has witnesses and his adversary has none, he can say that probabilities incur no responsibility, and that there would be no need of evidence, if an investigation according to the arguments were sufficient. (1376a)

Here, very plainly, the evidence of witnesses and of probabilities are contrasted, even when witnesses are understood to include absent

authorities. Even though probabilities are generally approved propositions, in other words, it would seem that they cannot be generally
approved propositions authored by individuals known to us—for then
they would constitute for these purposes the evidence of witnesses.
They seem rather to be something like proverbs in having a kind of
not merely anonymous but collective authorship. (In fact Aristotle has
already mentioned that proverbs too may be evidence, and it is easy to
see that many proverbs either have a probabilistic character or might
easily be recast as probabilities. For example, a proverb Aristotle has
just quoted—"Foolish is he who, having killed the father, suffers the
children to live" [1376a]—easily becomes "A child whose father is
murdered will [probably] seek revenge.")

This likeness between probabilities and proverbs suggests another
similarity, one between probabilities and at least some among the large
family of what Aristotle calls the commonplaces, those universal *topoi*
or lines of argument which may be applied to arguments in any field
(see especially 1358a). And again, their having only a general authorship and being in effect communal property are distinctive features.

But there is an important difference also between probabilities on
the one hand and proverbs and commonplaces on the other, for unlike
proverbs and the commonplaces, probabilities apparently have nothing
that we would call a literary distinction. It would no doubt be helpful
to us in deciding just what probabilities are if they were the kinds of
things people were in the habit of gathering into collections (like
proverbs). That there *are* no such collections suggests just how uninteresting and unmemorable probabilities are. No one is likely to spend
money on a book that tells us things like "the envious hate" or "the
beloved show affection." Even signs, which, we have seen, are for
several reasons easy to confuse with probabilities, are more likely
candidates for gathering into collections, for signs at least need to be
interpreted and may require a skillful, even a divine reader. But that the
envious hate or the beloved show affection seem true almost by
definition or to be *self*-evident—provable, that is to say, without the
need for recourse to any other evidence, be it that of witnesses or (to
complete Aristotle's interesting list of the kinds of evidence used in
forensic rhetoric) laws, contracts, oaths, or torture.

If probabilities are propositions that are virtually self-evident, it is as much as to say that what is probable is known by the generality of mankind or by common sense to be true because a probability is the next thing to a tautology—the *next* thing and not the thing itself because a tautology is a certainty. But if such is an accurate conclusion based upon a reading of what Aristotle has to say about probabilities in the *Rhetoric* and the *Prior Analytics,* it scarcely supplies a satisfactory definition, and it is one that seems to come uncomfortably close to Plato's scornful notion that the probable is for the rhetorician merely "that which commends itself to the multitude." It is in any case by no means clear just what propositions the generality of mankind *do* hold as common knowledge, and to say that the probable is that which people in general know to be what usually happens seems itself close to being a tautology or to beg the question. Only propositions that truly are tautologies seem safe candidates for inclusion in the family of generally approved propositions, but again the whole point of probabilities is that they have not attained the certainty of tautologies. Propositions that are uncertain are, by their very nature and as Aristotle notes, always subject to objection. And that which can be objected to does not seem a terribly good candidate for inclusion in the family of propositions generally approved. But of course that is exactly the problem, not only with probability, but with all inductions and nondemonstrative arguments; that problem is part, in fact, of what philosophers call the problem of induction: How does one understand the difference between certainty and uncertainty, and why is one ever justified in believing in an uncertainty?

WE ARE NOW in a position at least tentatively to be able to answer one important question, that of whether or not Aristotle's notion of the probable is something like ours. At first sight a definition that claims that probabilities are propositions does not seem to have much in common with our notion of probability, which is more apt to be seen as actually residing in the nature of real objects. (Thus we might connect the probability of a fair coin's turning up heads and tails a roughly equal number of times over the long run with actual, physical characteristics of the coin in question—precisely those characteristics that make it a fair coin.) We will see, however, that at least one modern philosopher has claimed something very like this: that there is no "probability" as such out there in the real world, but rather that what we call probability is simply an *attribute* of certain kinds of proposition. But before we worry too much about the ultimate validity of Aristotle's definition of the probable, we need also to ask whether his definition is in fact a good one in the sense of defining what he himself means by the probable. It is easy enough to see why he *wants* probabilities to be propositions: they can then be universals and perform all the functions of necessities. To make probabilities propositions of this kind means that arguments about uncertain matters of fact can be put on a footing just like that of the most rigorously logical abstract arguments: inductive logic therefore looks just like demonstrative logic (although with important qualifications attached, namely that probabilities do not *always* hold), and thus the whole of what will later be called the "problem of induction" is avoided, or at least pushed aside into a parenthetical qualification. Aristotle's other definitions look more familiar to us, and these I think suggest that he does mean something very like what we mean by the probable. To say that the probable is that which usually happens is of course perfectly consistent with modern usage, even if circular. (It even suggests the logic of mathematical probability: If it is what "usually" happens, how far away is the idea of counting how often in particular cases it actually does happen?) But more persuasive than his definitions are the contexts within which he puts probability to use. Probability as something to which we have resort in the face of inadequate evidence in deciding some question of fact—as in a courtroom—is obviously entirely consistent with our sense of probability.

TO SUM UP what Aristotle means by the probable in the *Prior Analytics* and the *Rhetoric*, we may say that a probability is a universal proposition that describes the way things usually happen. It is most often but not always true and that truth is recognized as such by the generality of mankind. More tautologically, the probable is what is generally provable/approvable. Probabilities are, moreover, so close to being self-evident as to need no statement. (In fact it is probably wiser to give no examples, because we may always by definition object to actual probabilities, whereas those we imagine without articulating are those we approve.)

In his other major discussion of the probable, in the *Poetics,* Aristotle takes the concept of the probable to be sufficiently well understood that no examples are in fact given. But if the *Poetics* does not seem explicitly to advance his definition of the probable, it does of course provide the inevitable starting point for literary discussions of the role of the proba-ble, for it is there that Aristotle makes clear just how central a role the probable ought to play in drama. He introduces the subject in the famous passage that begins chapter nine:

> From what has been said it is clear too that the poet's job is not
> to tell what has happened but the kind of things that *can* happen,
> i.e., the kind of events that are possible according to probability or
> necessity. For the difference between the historian and the poet is
> not in their presenting accounts that are versified or not versified
> . . . ; rather the difference is this: the one tells what has happened,
> the other the kind of things that can happen. And in fact that is why
> the writing of poetry is a more philosophical activity, and one
> to be taken more seriously, than the writing of history; for poetry
> tells us rather the universals, history the particulars. 'Universal'
> means what kinds of thing a certain person will say or do in accor-
> dance with probability or necessity, which is what poetic com-
> position aims at, tacking on names afterward; while 'particular' is
> what Alcibiades did or had done to him. Now in the case of
> comedy this has become clear; for they construct the plot with the
> use of probabilities, then (and not until then) assign whatever names
> occur to them, rather than composing their work about a partic-
> ular individual as the 'iambic' poets do. (1451a–1451b).[6]

Although Aristotle here takes for granted that his audience knows what he means by probability, that knowledge would seem to depend upon the discussion in the *Prior Analytics* and the *Rhetoric,* for he assumes that his audience understands that probabilities are universals. And their being universals is what determines their distinguishing importance for poetry as opposed to history, which is lesser because it can discuss merely what actually has happened, whereas poetry and philosophy speak theoretically, as it were, of the way "things can happen" and therefore in some sense speak of things as they ought to happen. Obviously probability here is held in extraordinarily high esteem, and Aristotle's concept is finally disclosed as very different in fact from Plato's notion in the *Phaedrus* of "that which commends itself to the multitude." If the probable has commended itself to the multitude, we might say, it is to both its and the multitude's credit, for there is no sense here of the probable as that which is a mere (and distorted) likeness of truth. The portrait of the truth that is embodied in the *likeli*-hood of probability is for Aristotle very clearly an accurate one.

But there are a couple of serious complications in this view of the probable as an accurate likeness of the truth, quite aside from the very controversial difficulties that theorists nowadays are fond of elaborating in any general mimetic theory. For one thing, the truth in question is itself universal rather than particular; it is not the truth of how actual people have actually acted, but the truth of how people ought to act "in accordance with probability or necessity." The probable picture is therefore to a degree idealized (or derealized). As Gerald F. Else puts it in his commentary on the *Poetics:*

> Our world, except in so far as we live the theoretical life of pure
> reason, is a realm of contingency and approximation. . . . That,
> in fact, is why Aristotle so carefully uses the double formula
> "according to probability or necessity" throughout the *Poetics;* for
> necessity can never be absolute in the sublunar world. Thus there
> are general principles, 'universals,' that are valid here, but they
> partake of the nature of the realm to which they belong. . . .
> ['Poetic'] can offer us . . . a view of the *typology of human nature,*
> freed from the accidents that encumber our vision in real life. It can
> show us "what kind of thing such and such a kind of man will
> naturally say or do" under given circumstances.[7]

Aristotle's *Poetics* are therefore very far from being what in a later age could be considered a realist manifesto, a fact that is surprising in Aristotle of course only when we come at the question from the modern viewpoint, which assumes that probability and realism are necessarily allied. Poetry and history differ in more than the empirical fact that one is about things that happen *not* to have occurred while the other is about things that happen *to* have occurred. Being about particularities that *have* occurred, history records the contingencies and accidents that, as Else puts it, "encumber our vision in real life," whereas poetry, being about universals, is about things that can happen but in fact—and apparently paradoxically—in all probability never will, because the events of real life do not unfold with the regularity of universals. In other words, probabilities seem to belong at once to the realms of the contingent *and* the necessary, for insofar as they are merely probable they are contingent, but insofar as they *are* universals, they have something of the character of the necessary. (Surely this is why in giving his examples, like "the envious hate," Aristotle leaves out the—to us—crucial qualification, "probably.")

This apparent paradox that probabilities are things that in all probability never will happen *exactly* as probability predicts helps to explain a famous and puzzling remark Aristotle quotes in the *Poetics* about the probable. At the end of a brief discussion of epic versus tragic plots, textually very difficult, Aristotle quotes a remark of Agathon's that "it is probable that many things should also happen contrary to probability" (1456a).[8] Else believes that Aristotle may be being ironic here and that in any case the quotation is "hardly more than a *jeu d'esprit*—interesting perhaps more as an added testimony to Aristotle's weakness for the witty Agathon than for its serious content," for in the *Rhetoric* Aristotle has shown that the idea is fallacious, "an 'apparent' or pseudo-enthymeme."[9] But Else seems mistaken in this, for in fact Aristotle has in the *Rhetoric* quarreled not with the reasoning but simply with the idea that the conclusion may be put forward as an absolute. While it is true that many (particular) things happen contrary to (universal) probabilities, this is not to say that it is probable that all improbabilities will occur: "That which is improbable will be probable. But not absolutely; but as, in the case of sophistical disputations, the argument becomes fallacious when the circumstances, reference, and manner are not added, so here it will become so owing to the probability being not probable absolutely but only in particular cases" (1402a). Far from exposing the fallacy of a witty paradox, Aristotle is showing what is the truth in it and is in effect stating what would today be considered an implication of the law of large numbers: probabilities assert themselves or become clear and attain regularity only in the long run, which means that only in large populations or after repeated trials does one see probabilities actually approaching the limits of predicted values. Only if I toss a coin many hundreds of times will I begin to see a frequency of heads that is really close to the predicted frequency of 50 percent. The implication relevant here is that for a small number of trials, it is probable that the frequency of heads will *not* be very close to 50 percent at all. It is probable, that is, that the improbable will occur. Equally importantly, Aristotle understands that what error there is in the argument occurs only when "the circumstances, reference, and manner are not added." This means not only that he is working with a concept of probability similar to ours, but further that he understands two important fundamentals of modern probability theory, that probability is always determined relative to actual evidence and that probabilities have no meaning except when we know what evidence has been drawn upon in determining them.

Aristotle's equally famous and puzzling prescription that "one should . . . choose impossibilities that are probable in preference to possibilities that are improbable" (1460a)[10] can also be seen as less paradoxical. The confusion is resolved when one recalls the idealized, universalized nature both of the probable and of the poetic. It is better in poetry to describe things that could not happen in fact but that seemingly could have or, better, that seemingly ought to have happened than it is to describe such contingent things as may (and under certain circumstances do) actually occur but which have not been shown to have any relation to the events described in a plot. Poetry should, that is, make at least apparent sense of the events it describes, whereas no such burden of coherence falls on the historian.

At this point, Aristotle really does seem to be returning to a notion of the probable very like that which Plato deplores in the rhetoricians —the probable as "that which commends itself to the multitude." Just prior to his introducing the idea of probable impossibilities, in fact, he has seemed to condone the use of logical fallacies that render specious causal connections probable. In the following chapter, concerned with the kinds of flaws critics may note in poetry, he appeals to what the generality of mankind believes as a justification of improbabilities in poetry:

> Generally speaking, we must judge the impossible in relation to its poetic effect, to what is better than reality, or to the general opinion (*doxa*). In regard to poetic effect, a persuasive or probable impossibility is preferable to an unpersuasive or improbable possibility. There are no such men as Zeuxis painted: "True," we say, "but the impossible is the better thing, and the ideal *should* surpass the real." The irrational or improbable (*alogos*) may be justified by reference to what men commonly believe and also on the grounds that the irrational sometimes turns out not to violate reason, just as "it is probable that many things should also happen contrary to probability." (1461b)[11]

While it is easy to see how a possibility may be improbable, it is hard to see how an impossibility may be made probable unless the "general opinion" or *doxa* is not, as in Plato's view, liable to be merely ignorant and wrong. But if it is ignorant and wrong, there seems a mistake in esteeming the general opinion as highly as Aristotle plainly does. For he writes as though "what men commonly believe" is somehow necessarily higher and better than what in actuality unfolds. There seems to be a mere sophistry, however, in saying that "the irrational sometimes turns out not to violate reason" or in arguing that what seems improbable is probable if it turns out to be what the general opinion believes, because probabilities are of course initially defined as generally approved propositions. But Aristotle's again quoting Agathon's remark suggests a more valid if elliptical reasoning in the idea. Just as a universal probability is likely in particular cases not to hold true, so too what reason or proportion *(logos)* seems to demand may in particular cases turn out not to be perfectly reasonable after all. Again it is a question of what evidence has been adduced. What *seems* unreasonable may turn out to be quite reasonable when we understand the actual circumstances of the case.[12]

These final comments that Aristotle makes about probability in the *Poetics* plainly leave us with few things we may say we know unambiguously about the concept of the probable, for in Aristotle's account probabilities have certain paradoxical properties that make them appear to fall between several stools at once. They are universals, and therein lies their central importance for poetry, for they belong to a higher reality than that of the actual events of ordinary life. But insofar as they operate in the actualities of the ordinary world they are only contingently true. They are generally approved propositions, and yet no catalogues of probabilities exist against which we could check our ideas of what the probable is. They are perhaps not so much *known* as true as *recognized* as true, as though they existed in an unconscious, pre-articulated space populated by *a priori* notions, and yet they have the quality too of empirical generalizations, and there appears to be nothing in their nature to prevent their being empirically derived. They may be used as evidence, and yet they are different from the evidence of actual witnesses, living or dead, so that if they have an authorship it is of a kind not merely anonymous but general. They appear therefore to be at once written and unwritten, authored and unauthored. And, finally, they sometimes seem to negate themselves, as when improbabilities are discovered to be probabilities, at least under particular circumstances.

Probabilities are thus in Aristotle's account ghostly things, easy to conceive of in a general and commonsensical sort of way (they are after all what most of us believe or know to be usually true) but liable to vanish when actual attempts to describe or specify them are made—liable to vanish, that is, into the gaps in logical space that open up between the tautological or self-evident on the one hand and the merely possible on the other, the gaps that still mark the unsolved "problem of induction."[13] For while Aristotle's account of the probable may seem unfinished and unsatisfactory, we shall learn that the major difficulties in it still lack resolution and that its essential ghostliness still haunts thinking about the probable. The fact that we can make sense even of the apparently most paradoxical references to probability in the *Poetics* suggests that Aristotle's notion of the probable and ours are not fundamentally different; the difficulties we have uncovered in his account testify not to the strangeness of his notion, but in fact to its similarity with ours, which turns out to be no less difficult.

Enough has by now been said about the probable, no doubt, to indicate some of the many fundamental and difficult notions with which it intersects—for example, the rational *(logos)*, the persuasive *(pithanon)*, opinion *(doxa, endoxon)*, likeness *(eikon)*—as well as to suggest those with which it contrasts—for example, the impossible *(adynaton)*, the improbable *(alogos)*, certain knowledge *(episteme)*. And there are important concepts closely related to probability and improbability that we have not yet touched upon at all, most notably the marvelous *(thaumaston)*, to which considerable attention is paid in the *Poetics* as well as in subsequent literary discussions about probability. A fuller reading of the probable in Aristotle would examine these related notions in some detail, but that fuller reading would not eliminate the undecidables we have thus far encountered, nor serve more securely to demonstrate the centrality of the concept not only in literature, but in any discourse that concerns itself with less than certain knowledge and representing the way the world is.

Chapter II

Hacking's Novelty

THE TEXT of Aristotle's *Poetics* was for all practical purposes lost throughout the Middle Ages. Its rediscovery at the end of the fifteenth century has been called by the most important literary historian of the period "the signal event in the history of literary criticism in the Italian Renaissance."[1] By the middle of the sixteenth century the text had become widely known and was beginning to be the central work for literary theory, which in some ways it remains to this day. The loss of the *Poetics* of course did not mean the suspension of all literary discussion of the probable or the verisimilar, but it is not until its recovery that discussions of the probable are once again brought to the heart of literary theorizing.

In the meantime, people did not cease to be aware that they believed things often for reasons that were less than certain—that their knowledge, to use the scholastic terminology of the Middle Ages' chief interpreter of Aristotle, St. Thomas Aquinas, was of the character of *opinio* rather than *scientia*. Those terms are of course the Latin translations of the Greek *doxa* and *episteme* and should recall to us the concept of the probable as defined by Aristotle in the *Prior Analytics* ("a generally approved proposition") and by Plato in the *Phaedrus* ("that which commends itself to the multitude"). Aquinas's ideas about knowledge both certain and uncertain are of course dominant in the high and late Middle Ages, and his ideas specifically about probable knowledge have fortunately been the object of a full study by Edmund F. Byrne. Byrne sums up some of the connotations that probability has for Thomas (and in Latin generally) by playing upon its paronyms:

[The] attribution of probability to an opinion has various connotations. In the first place, it refers to the authority of those who
accept the given opinion; and from this point of view "probability"
suggests *approbation* with regard to the proposition accepted and
probity with regard to the authorities who accept it. In the second
place, "probability" refers to the arguments which are presented in
favor of the opinion in question; and from this point of view it
suggests *provability,* that is, capacity for being proven (though not
necessarily demonstrated). In the third place, "probability" takes
on a somewhat pejorative connotation precisely insofar as the
proposition in question is *merely* probable; for, from this point of
view the proposition is only *probationary* and not strictly demonstrated as are propositions which are properly scientific.[2]

In light of what has already been said about Aristotle's concept of the
probable, it would seem that in the medieval mind the meaning of
probability has undergone not so much an evolution as a distillation,
coming quite narrowly to mean the quality acquired by propositions
that have met with general approval and to connote especially the
authority thereby acquired. It is thus a short step, as Ian Hacking points
out, from Thomas's idea of probability to the casuistry of *probabilism,*
which was the Jesuits' answer to the problem of what one does when
confronted by conflicting views in acknowledged authorities. And their
answer is simply that one can follow *any* opinion as long as one has
some written authority with which to support it, even in the face of
perhaps weightier authorities to the contrary. In practice, of course, this
meant that, in order to justify whatever doctrine one had already
decided to promote, one had only to find an authority, no matter how
obscure the source or feeble its merits, to lend credence to the doctrine.[3]

Hacking cites Byrne's account of Thomas and discusses probabilism
because the connection between probability and the approval of authority is crucial to the story he has to tell about why it is that the modern,
mathematicized theory of probability has to wait until the decade of the
1660s to be born. In fact, Byrne's account of Aquinas and the account

of probability in the present study are written slightly at cross purposes to Hacking's. But to see how and why that is so (as well as finally to understand why Hacking is reluctant to consider Aristotle), we shall have to look closely at the Hacking thesis. That will prove a rewarding effort, for the thesis is brilliant and engaging, even if for our purposes it will unfortunately prove necessary to correct and complicate it somewhat and perhaps in the process to diminish its elegance as story.

That last word is chosen carefully and is warranted by Hacking himself, who disarmingly writes after outlining his method and its presuppositions: "I do not ask any reader to swallow all this. The story told in what follows is of interest even if the methodology that led to it turns out to be silly."[4] This is more than simply a manner of speaking. Hacking is one of a number of philosophers—one thinks also of Richard Rorty—who with apparent modesty assume the guise of historians—that is, explicit storytellers—while making powerful conceptual contributions to their subjects. In their view, story and history are in various ways to be preferred to arguments written *sub specie aeternitate* and that pretend to a kind of foundational solidity now much in question. The modesty is by no means false, however, for it is not so much history that is exalted as philosophy that is brought down from the level of its traditionally privileged claims to possess knowledge that is uniquely well-grounded or uniquely accurate. Moreover, the reversion to story in both Rorty and Hacking signals an important recognition among philosophers trained in the tradition of Anglo-American analytic philosophy that it is hardly fruitful to do philosophy as though ideas existed independent of actual historical contexts and that understanding those contexts is necessary to the understanding of ideas. Because they are so centrally concerned with the status of knowledge, Rorty and Hacking are both deeply interested, though in somewhat different ways, by philosophy of science and particularly by those philosophers of science who, like Thomas Kuhn and Paul Feyerabend, are concerned with the historical status of theories and who are especially sensitive to the *discontinuities* between theories. Indeed, a fascination with discontinuities in knowledge (and in general) characterizes Rorty and Hacking and links them to a wider group of thinkers, especially such Continental philosophers as Jacques Derrida and Michel Foucault.[5]

Thus it ought not to be surprising that Hacking's thesis about the emergence of probability stresses discontinuity and novelty. And the subject of the modern, mathematicized theory of probability lends itself naturally to such emphasis because it is a theory, as has been long known, that does indeed emerge quite sharply and dramatically with the Port Royal *La Logique, ou L'art de Penser* of 1662, which reported Pascal's famous wager about the existence of God, with Huygens's *Ratiociniis in Aleae Ludo* of 1657, and with some even earlier attempts by Leibniz to invent a probability calculus not derived from games of chance. Like the differential calculus, in the invention of which Leibniz was also a major figure, mathematicized probability theory is one of those great human achievements independently arrived at by different people at almost the same time. The question for the historian is: Why not before that time? After briefly dealing with some clearly unsatisfactory answers, Hacking notes that the usual explanations

> All take for granted that there existed an intellectual object—a concept of probability—which was not adequately thought about nor sufficiently subject to mathematical reflection. So one asks, what technology was missing? What incentive was absent? These questions are appropriate only if the conceptual scheme of those earlier times had within it a concept of probability. If there was no such concept then all the questions are idle.[6]

And the answer for Hacking is that there was no such concept and that "our" concept of probability is consequently genuinely novel. The search therefore becomes one for the preconditions of probability, preconditions which "determined the very nature of this [novel] intellectual object, 'probability,' that we still recognize and employ and which, as philosophers, we still argue about." The search is therefore "more than an attempt at historical explanation," because, "the preconditions for the emergence of probability determined the space of possible theories about probability. That means that they determined, in part, the space of possible interpretations of quantum mechanics, of statistical inference, and of inductive logic."[7] The crucial development, the development that finally makes possible the modern concept of probability, is for Hacking a fundamental change that occurs in the nature of evidence. It is momentous not only because it makes modern probability theory possible, but because it makes possible as well the formulation of the notorious problem of induction. (That we have already met that problem in Aristotle, and specifically in the peculiarly double nature which probabilities possess for him, poised as they are between a realm of necessary universals and a realm of contingent particulars, should suggest one important way in which this study departs from Hacking's thesis; but let us follow its lead for the time being.)

The momentous change that Hacking sees as having occurred in the concept of evidence by the latter third of the seventeenth century is a movement away from the evidence of written authority—the evidence, in effect, of books—toward the evidence of the world itself —the evidence, as it were, of things. The old idea of evidence (and with it the old kind of probability) can be seen in its most debased form in the casuistry of probabilism; the new idea of evidence (and with it the new kind of probability) can be seen in full flower, of course, not only in the invention of the mathematical theory of probability, but in the invention of the institution of modern science and in the work of the great empiricists.

Described thus, Hacking's account may seem quite traditional; it looks very much like the account one learns in school of perhaps not the "invention" but the "discovery" of experimental method and its exposition by such heroes as Galileo, Bacon, and Mill. These are not Hacking's heroes, however, for they belong to a line of thinkers who have repeatedly sought certainty and hence tried to cast inductive thinking in the mold of deduction. This line of thought has repeatedly looked to the so-called high sciences of physics and astronomy for the ideal of scientific theorizing. But for Hacking, the heroes of the emergence of probability are the (by traditional lights) lowly alchemists and physicians who did not have their sights set on knowledge that was certain or arguments that were demonstrative or even on theory at all, but were content with the findings they were led to by experience and opinion. In such as the sixteenth-century alchemist Paracelsus we can see the perfect example of the transition from the evidence of books to the evidence of things and explore the mentality that makes such a transition possible, for in Paracelsus one sees not the fully developed idea of the evidence of things; rather one sees that idea emerging out of what today looks like a conflation of the idea of the evidence of books and the evidence of things. This conflation occurs in the idea of the sign, which includes for Paracelsus such things as "pictures, stones, herbs, words, . . . comets, similitudes, halos."[8] To the modern mind, these are a diverse lot. Hacking argues that they form for Paracelsus a natural kind, or group of things naturally related. What to the modern in speaking of the Book of Nature is a mere metaphor is therefore to the sixteenth-century alchemist, Hacking argues, a literal truth. Before skepticism about verbal or written authority finds a new faith in the evidence of things, in other words, it invests nature with not only the old authority and probability of testimony and the written word, but with something of their attributes as verbal entities as well. Hence the Book of Nature, like any book, is meant to be read, but to read it accurately one must know the language in which it is written. If the reader is Paracelsus, that language will be a crackpot, almost paranoid theory of signs, signatures, and similitudes fully worthy of its alchemical interpreter (Nature, he tells us, "made liverwort and kidneywort with leaves in the shape of the parts she can cure").[9] If the reader is Galileo (who, according to Hacking, picks up the alchemists' way of speaking as does just about everyone else in the sixteenth century), that language will turn out to be, in his famous phrase, "the language of mathematics." But in either case, for the high scientist as well as the low, a new way of understanding the world has opened up, and with it the possibility of a new kind of probability.

Whereas formerly only *people* could provide evidence (and so make one's belief in something more or less probable), now *anything* in the world could speak about the world and, most importantly, speak about things other than itself. Thus anything could point beyond itself (and so make one's belief in a something other than itself more or less probable). As Hacking is at pains to emphasize, however, the evidence of things is not merely the evidence of one's senses, and he effectively quotes J. L. Austin to make clear the distinction between evidence and simply seeing:

> The situation in which I would properly be said to have *evidence* for the statement that some animal is a pig is that, for example, in which the beast itself is not actually on view, but I can see plenty of piglike marks on the ground outside its retreat. If I find a few buckets of pig food, that's a bit more evidence, and the noises and smell may provide better evidence still. But if the animal then emerges and stands there plainly in view, there is no longer any question of collecting evidence; its coming into view doesn't provide me with more *evidence* that it's a pig, I can now just *see* that it is.[10]

Of course Hacking is not claiming that only in the seventeenth century did people learn how to infer the existence of pigs from piglike marks, noises, smells and other evidence; rather his claim is that it was the *concept* of such evidence that was lacking. "We do not deny that men in the Renaissance were able to take advantage of what we call the evidence," he writes. "I deny that their description of this practice was at all like our description, or even fits into any present category."[11] (Also excluded from the claim are such relatively distant cultures as the Sanskrit and, more notable but not surprising in view of his general disregard of Aristotle, the Greek.)[12] What stood in place of such a concept, again, was the kind of transitional concept represented by Paracelsus' notion of the sign, which includes both the testimony of people and of nature. By the time of the Port Royal *Logic* in 1662 (a critical text because in it for the first time probability was associated in print with a measurable quantity), a clearly conceptualized distinction is made between the testimony of people and the evidence of things. As the Port Royal *Logic* puts it in formulating a maxim for deciding in which of two possible occurrences to believe:

> *In order to judge of the truth of some event and to decide whether or not to believe in its occurrence, the event need not be considered in isola-*

tion—such as a proposition of geometry would be; but rather all the circum-
stances of the event, both internal and external, should be considered. I
call internal circumstances those which belong to the event itself;
external circumstances, those which pertain to the persons by
whose testimony we are led to believe in the event's occurrence. If
the circumstances of the event are such that like circumstances
are rarely accompanied by falsity, we are naturally led to believe
that the event is true.[13]

On the one hand, external circumstances, Hacking notes, are equivalent to the old authority of books, the testimony of people; the recognition of internal circumstances, on the other hand, signifies the new
concept of the evidence of things, the evidence of "those [circum-
stances] which belong to the event itself." This distinction is made
possible once one has recognized a distinction between conventional
and natural signs—once one recognizes, in other words, that not all
names are necessarily or divinely true, but that some are contingently
and humanly given. Those that are conventional correspond to the
evidence of people; those that are natural correspond to the evidence of
things, and lead one to look for inner evidence in a language that may
be utterly unlike the ordinary—like Galileo's language of the universe,
mathematics. Thus for the Port Royal *Logic,* too, the evidence of
things can under some circumstances be measured and thus be made
the subject of mathematical calculation.

In writing the story of the preconditions of probability, Hacking has
a very narrow path to follow. His Foucauldian taste for discontinuity
moves him to make people before and after the invention of the
evidence of things look like beings very different from one another
indeed—and also serves to make his story much more interesting than
it otherwise would be, for without the discontinuity there would
hardly be any drama to it; the invention of the mathematical theory
would, rather than being truly epoch-making, simply mark another of
innumerable stages in the progress of reason. But too much discontinuity is also for the purposes of his story a dangerous thing. Indeed, the
traditional accounts of the invention of the mathematical theory of
probability may be said to assume such an enormous discontinuity in

the history that they do not even bother with what comes before 1660, the so-called prehistory of probability having no relevance at all (beyond the mere and unfortunate lexical similarity) to its history proper. Thus a classic expositor of the mathematical theory of probability like Richard von Mises warns his readers against confusing the everyday sense of probability with its technical sense and writes that "it is unfortunate that most languages have no specific word for probability in its scientific sense but only popular terms like Wahrscheinlichkeit, probability, probabilité."[14] As a historian of the philosophy of language (as well as a historian of probability—he is perhaps most widely known for his book *Why Does Language Matter to Philosophy?*),[15] Hacking understands the unsatisfactoriness of such an emphatic and seemingly clear-cut distinction between ordinary and technical senses of words. And without *some* continuity between old and new senses of probability, he not only has no story to tell, but no place to locate a space out of which the new concept might emerge. Thus he works under the constraint of maintaining a more or less constant but also more or less unobtrusive tension between the similarities and differences in old and new senses of probability. That his account proves so satisfying testifies to his gifts as a storyteller and his ability to sustain such a delicate rhetorical task.

We are now in a somewhat better position to understand Hacking's apparent underestimation of Aristotle: it may not be a real underestimation at all, but rather an underplaying for the sake of the story. As the reading of Aristotle's concept of the probable offered above should make evident, the probable can for him by no means simply be equated with the authority of books. Indeed, in the discussion of testimony in the *Rhetoric,* we have seen, the evidence of authors is specifically contrasted with the evidence of probability. For that reason if for no other (and presently it will become apparent that there are others), Aristotle doesn't fit into Hacking's account at all neatly, but looks like an anticipation of more modern notions. Hacking has a similar problem with a figure like Jerome Cardano, author of the first book about chance and gambling written in the middle of the sixteenth century, but not published for more than a hundred years, in 1663.[16]

That his work contains by Hacking's own account "all the germs of a reflective study of chance" is undeniable, but for Hacking that fact does not seriously damage his claim that "probability emerged only in 1660." The salient point is that Cardano's work had no impact for more than a hundred years. In a sense, therefore, he becomes the exception that proves the rule. The failure of the rest of the world to recognize and take up the concept when it *did* effectively emerge in Cardano might itself demonstrate that the necessary space for the concept of probability had not yet opened in general discourse, and because Hacking's study "is not of great men but rather of an autonomous concept," Cardano, like Aristotle, remains peripheral to the main plot.[17]

A number of writers have pointed to quite a large body of evidence that apparently undermines the Hacking thesis. (There was a certain amount of such evidence already collected before Hacking's account, especially in articles by S. Sambursky and O. B. Sheynin.)[18] The most important of these writers are Ivo Schneider (in his paper "Why Do We Find the Origin of a Calculus of Probabilities in the Seventeenth Century?"), Daniel Garber and Sandy Zabell (in their article "On the Emergence of Probability"), and Douglas Patey (who adds a cogent appendix, "The Foucault-Hacking Hypothesis," to his *Probability and Literary Form* as well as a large number of examples of the modern concept of probability in use before 1660.)[19] Each of these writers is able to adduce a substantial number of examples that show there is in fact a concept of internal evidence before the Port Royal *Logic*. Hacking in his rebuttal to Schneider's paper (presented at the same conference) has indeed shifted his ground somewhat, admitted a number of the oversimplifications of the thesis, but also claimed that there is less disagreement between Schneider and himself than would at first appear.[20] It would take us too far afield to explore the criticisms of the Hacking thesis in great detail, but a couple of points need to be noted.

The first is that everyone is agreed that something very important does happen around 1660, because it is indeed then that the first calculations begin to be made and that more generally the concept of probability is, as we have seen Hacking put it, "upon every pen."[21] Even if, in other words, one can adduce all sorts of examples that suggest the modern concept of probability prior to 1660, the fact remains that in some important ways these remain outside the mainstream until then, for it is not until then that they organize themselves into a relatively coherent discourse in which the connections between various uses of probability become apparent or in which it seems commonsensical to apply numbers to probabilities. The second point is that everyone also seems to be agreed that a crucial element in the change that occurs around 1660 has to do with chance. Hacking himself evidently realizes this in referring in the title of his rebuttal to the "Erosion of Determinism." In other words, it may not be so much the concept of probability itself that emerges in a novel way around 1660, but rather a new concept of chance—or at least a new relationship between the concepts of probability and of chance.[22] As virtually all of Hacking's critics point out, Aristotle distinguishes between what happens according to probability and what happens according to chance—as should come as no surprise given our analysis in chapter one—for probabilities partake of the universal, while chance occurrences (such as history is full of) are accidental and by their very nature not intelligible to reason.[23] What makes the mathematics of probability possible therefore might be, from one point of view, the notion that chance itself obeys regular laws (in the long run, if not in the short run) or, from another point of view, that the probable does not in fact partake of the universal, but itself falls under the aegis of chance. From the one point of view, chance events become for the first time analyzable by reason; from the other, a much wider range of phenomena now are seen as coming under the aegis of the merely random—hence "the Erosion of Determinism."

I don't believe that the criticisms that have been made of the Hacking thesis need significantly diminish its value for us, for two reasons. This is chiefly because the critics themselves have written out of a point of view at least as oversimplified as Hacking's in his more flamboyant moments. That is, they have tended to overlook the extent to which Hacking wants to have the question of the novelty of probability both ways, wants in other words to keep in play both the

continuities and the discontinuities between the concepts of probability before and after 1660. Hacking himself of course has allowed
for something very like the modern concept of probability both in
Aristotle as well as in Sanskirt sources.[24] His point really is therefore
not that the modern concept is entirely novel, but rather that it seems
entirely novel given the close association of probability and opinion and
given the pronounced authority of the evidence of books in the Middle
Ages and Renaissance. The thesis is surely right in connecting the
emergence of the modern concept of probability with the general shift
in authority that occurs in the latter part of the seventeenth century,
even if we do find many instances of the concept of internal evidence
long before then, and even if we find many instances of apparently
scholastic senses of probability long after.

IT MAY BE HELPFUL—indeed, necessary—here to look back at
the ground we have covered thus far, for the course we have followed
has not been especially easy. We began our examination of the literary
and extraliterary concept of probability by looking at the concept in
Aristotle, who in this as in so many matters provides the first discussion of any length and the seminal discussion for literary criticism.
What we found was a concept of great complexity which resists clear
definitions beyond such question-begging ones as the "likely." Indeed,
the concept seems intuitively clear as long as one does *not* try to define
it, and rather than define it we defined a set of problems. These have to
do with kinds of statements or knowledge about the way the world is
that fall just barely short of certainty and partake of qualities both of the
universal and particular, kinds of statements or knowledge that look
proverbial, have close connections with signs, and seem at once to
belong to everyone and to no one, to be written and un-written. After
looking at the sometimes seemingly paradoxical prescriptions that
Aristotle makes about the use of probability in literature, we looked
briefly at how probability appeared to Aquinas, Aristotle's chief
commentator in the Middle Ages, and thus at how it appeared at the

dawn of the Renaissance. There we found that the concept had resolved itself very largely into the kind of less-than-certain knowledge
or opinion that is based upon the authority of the written word. At
that point we took up the argument of Ian Hacking, which wants to
answer the question why it is that the modern, mathematicized theory
of probability should be born, conceptually virtually whole and in a
variety of separate texts, suddenly around 1660. And we saw that
Hacking's answer is that only then did the critical concept of the
"evidence of things," as opposed to the evidence of books and as developed initially by such lowly empirics as the alchemists in their concept
of the sign, come into general discourse. We saw too how the rhetorical needs and methodology of Hacking's story led him to play down
Aristotle's discussion and indeed all percursors of the modern concept
before 1660 or thereabouts.

Before we can turn to a rigorous analysis of what relevance the
modern concept of probability has for literature in general and the
novel in particular, however, we need to know more about exactly
what concept of probability it is that emerges with the invention of the
evidence of things. And specifically, we need to consider the question
of whether the word *probability* properly embraces one concept or
many, for if many, then it may be that the question of fictional probability is really quite separate from the evolution of the mathematical
concept.

It should come as no great surprise to discover that the modern
notion has proven philosophically as difficult to define as Aristotle's
and has occasioned very considerable debate. Like Aristotle's it remains
tied to the logical gap between what is deductively or demonstratively
certain and what is merely possible. (That gap becomes known in
philosophy, where today it still looms large, as the problem of induction. It was first formulated—though not, of course, with explicit
reference either to induction or to probability—by Hume in *A Treatise
of Human Nature* as part of his celebrated discussion of causality. There
the problem takes the form of a skeptical doubt about whether one is
ever justified in believing that something may happen merely because
similar things have happened in the past.)[25] And among the difficulties

about induction there are the questions whether there is one kind of inductive logic or many and one kind of probability or many. Depending upon which philosophers one listens to, in fact, there are several ways of counting the concept or concepts of probability. Some would have it that there is no concept of probability, some that there really only is one (and lots of erroneous ones), some that there is one (with lots of senses), and some that there are many, having little of substance to do with one another. Hacking is among those who hold—with some equivocation—that there is one fundamental concept, but that it embraces multiple senses; because this study will follow him in this and because we have already come quite a ways in the company of his ideas, it will be convenient to discuss his account of this question by way of introducing us to some other views among contemporary philosophers.

Chapter III

Ambiguity and the Modern Concept
of Probability

HACKING devotes a whole chapter to what he calls the "duality" of probability.[1] Somewhat more evocatively, he calls the modern concept "Janus-faced," a characterization which underscores his belief that the two distinct faces of probability have a fundamental unity. He writes, "On the one side it [probability] is statistical, concerning itself with stochastic laws of chance processes. On the other side it is epistemological, dedicated to assessing reasonable degrees of belief in propositions quite devoid of statistical background."[2] Thus the modern concept is interested on the one hand (the stochastic, statistical, or aleatory hand) in such problems as are posed typically by games of chance and the business of insurance (which the new mathematics of probability for the first time could put on a scientific footing). It is interested in such questions as, What are my chances of throwing a seven with a pair of dice? or, What are my chances of living beyond age sixty-eight? On the other hand (the epistemological or inductive hand), it is interested in the degree of belief one is justified in investing in propositions about which one cannot possibly gather statistical evidence; typically and most urgently in the seventeenth and eighteenth centuries, these were religious propositions about the existence of God. But more recently, under the aegis of decision theory, epistemological probability has interested itself in any proposition about the future that may affect one's choice among actions.

48

Statistical and epistemological probability statements of course have in common that they take the form of propositions modified by the word *probably:* thus I can say, "Probably I'll live till seventy," or, "Probably God exists." But although it is easy in ordinary language to cast such different problems in one another's usual form (What degree of faith should I put in the proposition that I'll live beyond sixty-eight? or, What are the odds that there is a God?), as soon as one begins to think seriously about how to answer such questions they do begin to look different indeed, because in the one case I can look for stable statistical frequencies to draw inferences from while in the other I have no such data to draw on.

What makes Hacking believe that they share a fundamental unity is first of all that such problems suddenly begin to be posed *together* around 1660 by many different people, many of whom had had no contact with one another. In such a representative figure as Leibniz, both kinds of probability emerge simultaneously; but perhaps more persuasive is that those who apparently write from one side of probability often fall into the language of the other. As Hacking notes,

> The Port Royal *Logic* . . . ends with a discussion of reasonable belief and credibility. Graunt's *Observations,* published in the same year, 1662, is entirely dedicated to demography and the analysis of stable frequencies [being "the first extensive set of statistical inferences drawn from mortality records"]. Yet the *Logic* has whole sentences of exactly the same form as are found in Graunt.[3]

Moreover, the subsequent history of philosophical thinking about probability repeats the pattern: no matter how hard philosophers try to keep the statistical and epistemological sides of probability well separated, they keep coming back to one another.

In the twentieth century, the most influential proponent of multiple senses has been Rudolf Carnap, who sees two quite distinct concepts of probability, which he calls "probability$_1$" and "probability$_2$" and which are equivalent to the two sides of Hacking's dual notion, probability$_1$ signifying "rational credibility" (or epistemological probability) and probability$_2$ signifying "limiting relative frequency of occurrence" (or statistical probability).[4] But unlike Hacking's two sides, Carnap's two terms are meant to represent truly multiple meanings and do not belong at all to the same coin. Max Black has argued that Carnap's distinction "proves, upon examination, to be based solely upon the different modes of verification of two probability assertions, one held to be a priori, the other empirical," and that therefore "there seem to be no compelling reasons for recognizing radically distinct senses of probability."[5] And, like Hacking, we may question why, if the two concepts are fundamentally different, the same word clings to both: "Philosophers seem singularly unable to put asunder the aleatory and epistemological side of probability. This suggests that we are in the grip of darker powers than are admitted into the positivist ontology. Something about the concept of probability precludes the separation which, Carnap thought, was essential to further progress."[6] But the relationship between the two sides of probability is for Hacking rather more complex than Black's relationship simply between two methods of verification. Elsewhere Hacking wonders: "Out of what historical necessity were these readily distinguishable families of ideas [the dual sides of probability] brought into being together and treated as identical? . . . Why all these frantic gropings for a terminology to make distinctions?"[7] That questions about epistemological and aleatory probability emerged together historically is a sign of their historically determined, fundamental unity, as is the fact that in English (as in French, German, Italian, and so on) a single word clings to both kinds; that philosophers from the seventeenth century on have repeatedly tried to distinguish them is a sign of their (also fundamental?) duality. It is possible to read Hacking here as equivocal, but recalling the rhetoric of his argument will help provide the answer why, if not clear up a real conceptual difficulty. It has to do again, like his playing down of Aristotle, with the whole enterprise of showing a new concept of probability emerging out of an old and the consequent problem of continuity/discontinuity, the need to sustain a tension between the similarity and difference of the old and new concepts.

Although they are different, there is a clear kinship between the "old" probability derived from the authority of people and the epistemological side of the "new" probability derived from the authority of things. The difference is in the kind of evidence which confers probability; the kinship is in the identity of the kinds of propositions and the kinds of credibility in question. Probability that is aleatory is the kind that seems novel, at least in the sense that until around 1660 nobody could solve practical problems having to do with gambling, insurance, annuities, and the like, whereas soon after their solutions were almost common knowledge. (The novelty in question here is first of all a matter of seeing a new sort of evidence; the mathematicization of probability is itself a consequence of that new concept of evidence.) But if Hacking were to argue simply that once upon a time there was a kind of probability that was epistemological and then in the latter part of the seventeenth century there was invented another kind of probability that is aleatory, he would then have put himself virtually in the camp of all those more traditional writers about the mathematical theory who assume that nothing that happened before 1660 or so matters very much. If he is to have much of a story to tell at all, if there are any such things as the preconditions for probability to locate and explore, then again the old and new probabilities must have a good deal in common as well as much in difference.

Putting this equivocation largely aside, then, we may say that Hacking's account is roughly as follows. There is a concept of probability, and, like all concepts, it exists only in historically realized substantiations. While there certainly existed in classical Greece and in ancient India (among other times and places) concepts of the probable similar to our modern one, as a matter of historical fact the concept of the probable available at the beginning of the Renaissance looked by and large very little like ours because it had as a necessary aspect its relation to the credibility of propositions based upon the authority of the people who had authored them. Lacking in the concept, again by and large, was the modern notion of the evidence of things, especially the evidence of things that behave in a random, accidental sort of way. With the invention or reinvention of that concept, it became possible to ascribe probability according not to authority but to the way the world itself actually is. This new way of ascribing probability was at first achieved through the transitional concept of the sign, which among supposedly lowly alchemists like Paracelsus included both the evidence of books and the evidence of things. Only later does the concept of the evidence of things become fully distinguished from (and valued over) that of the evidence of books. Therefore one would subsequently look for probability not so much in the testimony of people as in the random arrangement and behavior of things in nature. Depending on one's point of view (and it is here that the equivocation comes in), around 1660 either the concept of probability underwent its most momentous revolution or a genuinely novel concept of probability emerged, but in either case the new sense emerged very much out of the old.

Modern theorists of probability who believe in either one concept or multiple concepts can for the most part easily be understood within categories already made familiar to us by Hacking. We have already seen that Carnap, most influential of the proponents of multiple concepts, distinguishes his probability$_1$ and probability$_2$ along lines very closely resembling those of Hacking's two "sides." The proponents of a single concept of probability similarly tend to favor one or another of those sides. Today there are three important schools of thought among theorists of probability. There are first of all those who follow John Venn and Richard von Mises and what is often known as the frequency theory, which corresponds to aleatory probability. It holds that the only philosophically sound statements of probability one can make are those about the behavior of large populations of things or people that over the long run achieves statistical stability: that tends to show observable, measurable, and predictable frequencies, in other words. Secondly, there are those who follow Leonard J. Savage and Bruno de Finetti and what is often called "personal probability" or the subjective theory, which corresponds to epistemological probability insofar as it holds that all probability statements are really statements about the speaker's own confidence or degree of belief in the utterance. Probability thus becomes a property not of objects out there but a property of a believing subject; the task of such a subjective theory then becomes how to establish principles of coherence or rationality that are narrow enough to entail similar conclusions of probability among different subjects, but not so broad as to allow us to call any merely idiosyncratic opinion a probable one. And there is a third school, which came in and out of fashion somewhat earlier than the subjectivists' and that also roughly corresponds to what Hacking calls the epistemological side of probability. Its main proponents in this century have been Maynard Keynes, Harold Jeffreys, and, again, Carnap. Its goal has been to found a theory that understands probability as a purely logical attribute of propositions, or rather as a logical relation between a hypothesis (the probability statement proper) and the evidence for it.[8]

Each of these schools has its obvious attractions, and indeed most of us will find satisfying intuitions in each. It is easy to see that there is a built-in tendency for coins and dice to turn up each of their faces an equal number of times over the long run. It is easy to see too that plenty of other physical objects, like chromosomes and indeed even people and groups of people, display such tendencies and that it is these tendencies that have made possible, for example, many of the successes of modern biology and the social sciences. It is no less easy to see how saying, "Probably we will have fine weather for the picnic," expresses a speaker's confidence that a planned outing will take place. Problems come about largely only when one realizes that apparently contradictory claims are being made by competing theories. How can one reconcile the idea of probability as a degree of belief (as it is for the subjectivists) with the idea of probability as a literally physical property (as it is for some frequentists)? As Max Black puts it:

> None of the chief types of interpretation of probability now in favor can be accepted as wholly satisfactory. One reason may be that an acceptable philosophy of probability is called upon to perform a number of tasks that are hard to reconcile: to show why some probability judgments are a priori whereas others are contingent; to provide a firm basis for a calculus of probability while recognizing probability judgments that are incorrigibly imprecise; to account for and to defend the connection between "rationality" and specifiable degrees of confidence in conclusions following with

probability from given premises; and, above all, to show how and why it is justifiable to act on probabilities.[9]

There is, however, another way out of the problem, one offered by another group of theorists of probability: those who argue that there is in a sense *no* philosophically sound meaning of probability.

The ideas of these philosophers don't fall along the lines of Hacking's argument quite so neatly as do those of the frequentists and subjectivists. In general, their analyses begin with the common-sense and ordinary-language aspects of probability, and they consequently lack Hacking's sensitivity to history and historical change. But they are sufficiently sensitive to the nuances of typical probability statements in ordinary language and sufficiently close to Hacking in his belief in the fundamental relatedness of probability statements—in contrast to Carnap, say—that we cannot afford to overlook them. Max Black is himself perhaps among them, and so certainly is Stephen Toulmin, who has interestingly argued what we may call the no-probability theory. He believes that philosophers ask the wrong questions when they ask, "What *is* Probability?" or, "What are probability-statements *about*?" Why wrong?

> In the first place, the abstract noun 'probability'—despite what we learnt at our kindergartens about nouns being words that stand for things—not merely has no tangible counterpart, referent, *designatum* or what you will, not merely does not name a thing of whatever kind, but is a word of such a type that it is nonsense even to talk about it as denoting, standing for, or naming anything. . . . There can be probability-statements about the evening's weather, about my expectation of life, . . . the correctness of a scientific theory, the identity of a murderer—in fact, any subject on which one can commit oneself, with reservations, to an opinion. . . .
>
> Conversely, there is no special thing which all probability-statements must be about, simply in virtue of the fact that they are probability-statements.[10]

In other words, we make an error in assuming that because we have an adverb *probably* there must be some*thing* referred to by the noun (*probability*) we have happened to make out of it. As J. N. Findlay puts it:

> Our tendency to speak of 'the probabilities' or 'the chances', in the objective detached manner in which we speak of 'the elections' or 'the tides', arises only when we begin to see how the pulls and counterpulls of evidence depend for their force, in regular fashion, on the objective considerations which are brought forward as reasons, and that they are therefore themselves after a fashion imposed on us from without, and so can be credited with a *sort* of objectivity.[11]

But this particular way out of the problem of course offers no final solution. There are as many ways for the proponents of the no-probability theory to disagree about what *probably* means as there are for the proponents of probability theory to disagree about what "probability" is. Toulmin says that "to say 'Probably *p*' is to assert guardedly, and/or with reservations, that *p;* it is *not* to assert that you are tentatively prepared to assert that *p*."[12] The distinction may at first seem vanishingly fine, but in fact it repeats the quarrel with the subjectivists, for in the former case (of making a guarded assertion) one is saying something, even if with reservation, about the world out there, whereas in the latter case (of being tentatively prepared to make an assertion) one stops short of saying something about the world out there and really says something only about the state of one's own mind. And Toulmin is quarreling as well with another well-known philosopher of probability, William Kneale, who earlier had subscribed to the belief—consonant with our discussion of the etymology of *probability*—that in ordinary language the probable is "such as a rational man would approve as a basis for practical decisions."[13] To define probability as an attribute of certain sorts of propositions in this way may recall Aristotle's definition of probabilities, for Toulmin's description of the adverb *probably* as expressing a reservation about an otherwise seriously asserted proposition looks very much like Aristotle's description of probabilities as universals that assert the way things happen, albeit with the reservation that they may happen otherwise. And we shall see too that Toulmin's definition bears a remarkable similarity to a definition to be met with later on, not of probabilities, but rather of fictions.

One of Toulmin's aims is to get us out of what he calls the "labyrinth" of probability, the hopeless historical tangle of competing arguments about what probability is.[14] But as we have seen, to shift the problem to the question of what the logically prior *probably* means scarcely helps us to find our bearings among the competing arguments any more surely. Some of the quarrels just discussed are reminiscent of debates between subjectivists and frequentists; some of them are reminiscent of the much earlier discussions in Aristotle and Aquinas. And as Hacking points out, those debates between frequentists and subjectivists themselves have clear origins in the earliest days of the modern theory of probability: "In the past 300 years there have been plenty of theories about probability, but anyone who stands back from the history sees the same cycle of theories reasserting itself again and again. . . . Many a reader may begin to have a feeling of *déjà vu*."[15] (It is in fact just because of this cyclical nature of the history of probability that Hacking's account is really about much more than the beginnings of modern probability theory. It is in effect an account of all modern probability theory, but he can end his account with Hume's formulation of the problem of induction in 1737, for by then all the major ideas about probability had received their initial articulations.)

It is not our task to settle the competing claims among theorists of probability. More important is our seeing that the unoriginal but plausible reasons I have put forward why the various ideas that go under the name of *probability* all do indeed belong to the same conceptual family. This means that quantitative probability and qualitative probability are of a kind. We have made use of a plausible historical account of the emergence of probability—Ian Hacking's account, which I have revised to rectify its playing down of Aristotle and other precursors of the modern concept of probability. Our chief interest in this has been in surveying the *range* of ideas that have historically been involved in accounts of probability, because what will turn out to be the case is that it is precisely this range of ideas that is reembodied in the form and interests of the novel; whatever meaning that fact might have for philosophy is not here in question.

With this sketch of modern theories of probability, our exploration of the purely philosophical questions raised by probability is completed. There will be occasion to fill in some of the details of that sketch later on, but by now the general outlines and wide importance of those philosophical treatments (and perhaps too the peculiarity of their failure to receive attention outside philosophy) should be well established. We may in any case now turn more or less exclusively to the consequences that all of this has for literature, for while I have paid close attention to the *Poetics* of Aristotle, I have as yet to say anything of the history of probability in literature after him.

Part Two

Literary Probability after Aristotle

Chapter IV

In the Renaissance

BECAUSE we are interested in the logical space occupied by the concept of probability, it becomes important to know if that space remains fundamentally the same for literary theorists and practitioners in the Renaissance and up through the period of the rise of the novel. Our need is not for a finely detailed history of the vicissitudes of literary probability in the Renaissance and after, and our interest is not in questions like, What sort of part does probability play in Castelvetro's poetics? or, What kinds of things exactly does Tasso find credible? The significant question is not who says what about literary probability at a given moment so much as what range of statements is possible. It is important to know what aspects of probability are available or apparent in the periods before the rise of the novel to see, in a later section, if the new awareness of those aspects sheds light on the history of the novel. Having by now delineated a range of ideas embodied in the concept of probability implicit already in Aristotle, I want to discover whether any large changes occur in the contour of that range during the Renaissance, a period of obvious importance for the history of literary theory and of course also the critical period for Hacking's theory of the emergence of the modern concept of probability. Therefore we face two big questions: what does literary probability look like in the period just before the rise of the novel, and how do developments in literary theory parallel those in the philosophy of probability?

The appropriate place to begin is among the literary theorists, who took up the *Poetics* first at the end of the fifteenth century and continued to comment upon it throughout the Renaissance, for it is among these that Aristotle's ideas first passed into general literary discourse, and it is their discussions that form the background of discussions of probability among the early novelists.

Of course questions having to do with probability and improbability in Renaissance literary theory are central, and Baxter Hathaway in his important study *Marvels and Commonplaces: Renaissance Literary Criticism* has argued that such questions are indeed more than that; they are for him definitive of literary criticism in the period.[1] One could, in addition, no doubt plausibly argue that the sudden coming to prominence and then dominance of Aristotle's text—it never was technically "lost"—was motivated by a newly felt need to explore a theory of probabilities in poetry that accompanied the emergence of the modern concept: we are talking, after all, about a period identical with the heyday of Paracelsus.

There is first of all to be noted the sheer *amount* written in the Renaissance about the probable and especially about those concepts most often connected by contrast with it, chiefly the marvelous and the impossible. In theorist after theorist one finds long lists of the things that may be accounted marvelous but that should nevertheless be allowed in tragedy and narrative poems. Mazzoni in his *Della difesa della Comedia di Dante,* after apparently having wound up his discussion of the marvelous and the verisimilar, goes on for more than two hundred further pages to talk about impossibilities that may be made credible and that thus are allowable. In all, he lists by Hathaway's count "some thirty-four different ways by which the marvelous can be made credible."[2] And this is not an extraordinarily extensive treatment for a critic of the time. In the likes of Tasso, Castelvetro, Patrizi, and Buonamici one finds similarly exhaustive discussions. The marvelous is of course not identical with the improbable; indeed, in some cases marvels may have close associations with the probable. The *marvelous* is related etymologically to the *admirable* and thus partakes of the approbation that attaches to probability. It is cognate too with *miracle* (and of course in Renaissance discussions examples of the marvelous are often miracles in fact), but miracles are often associated with signs, which we have seen to be closely related to probabilities in Aristotle. Indeed, the most common New Testament word for *miracle* is *semeion*. But in spite of these important and sometimes curious associations of the marvelous and the probable, which are made especially complicated by the changing standards of credibility that follow the giving way of the pagan marvelous to the Christian marvelous, it is safe to say that in Renaissance discussions the *marvelous* signifies something that is regularly thought of as providing a counterbalance to the probable and therefore as something essentially equivalent to the *im*probable.

Although there are considerable disagreements in detail and there are apparently more substantial disagreements in theory between those who lean more towards Plato, Neoplatonism, or Aristotle, there is substantial agreement in the kinds of advice given about the relations between the marvelous and the impossible on the one hand and the probable, credible, or verisimilar on the other: epic and tragedy both call for some kind of mixture of the marvelous and the probable, or what was widely known as the "marvelous credible," a phrase that descends from Aristotle's discussion of probable impossibles. Tasso's formulation is representative: "The poem reaches the highest degree of perfection when these two things [the marvelous and verisimilitude] are joined together, and they may be conjoined in various ways." He is thinking here of the marvelous "as consisting," Bernard Weinberg tells us, "of those events which do not enter into natural probability."[3]

Why all of this interest in marvels? The most general answer has of course to do with the problems posed by the Christian marvelous—the need somehow to adapt pagan mythologies and poetics and all the marvels they entailed to orthodox Christian belief. Aristotle's discussions in the *Poetics* about probable impossibles and impossible probables were themselves difficult enough to leave plenty of room for debate. For the most part eager to follow Aristotle's prescriptions, the Renaissance theorist was at some pains to discover just what those prescriptions were. As we have seen, they are in fact by no means easy to understand today; undoubtedly they were even less easy to understand during the Renaissance, when for the most part it had not yet occurred to commentators that there might have been some significant evolution in the operative concepts in the intervening nineteen centuries. The probable and the marvelous were interesting to the Renaissance theorist, then, in part because they were problematic to a Christianity trying to accommodate a pagan tradition, in part because they were interesting to the greatest classical authority on poetry, and above all because they were not well understood.

Among the things that made them difficult concepts beyond their intrinsic difficulty was that Aristotle himself seemed to be making contradictory prescriptions concerning them. On the one hand, he had written that the poet was to portray events that were made possible by probability or necessity. On the other, he had plainly allowed for events that were marvelous and indeed even impossible and had begun to distinguish between, for example, the kinds of marvels that were allowable in epic and the kinds allowable on the stage. That Aristotle never went very far in exemplifying what he meant by marvels or probabilities, however, only compounded the problem—and left wide open to the Renaissance theorist the possibility of endlessly enumerating their varieties of manifestation.

Also among the difficulties encountered by the Renaissance theorist was the importance that had come to be placed upon Plato's distinctions (made in the *Sophist*) between icastic and fantastic imitations, the former roughly meaning imitations of the world out there and the latter roughly meaning imitations of what the imagination has dreamt up. For Aristotle, the object of the poet's imitation, of course, had plainly been things out there—chiefly human character and action. Plato's distinction complicates the question about the marvelous because when one conceives of what the imagination may dream up as a possible object for imitation by poetry, one may in the process have introduced a whole new set of criteria for what constitutes a marvel, because what is marvelous in the real world may not be marvelous in imagination. And in the same process one may have vastly lengthened the list of manifestations of the marvelous.

What those lists reveal is that there was in the Renaissance no widely accepted standard of credibility against which to measure the marvelous. Consider, for example, the three species of the marvelous according to Castelvetro, which are listed by Hathaway as "(1) animals without reason, (2) men who commit crimes intentionally, and (3) men who do horrible things by accident or against their will." This is certainly a strange list, and although there turn out to be some thoughtful criteria associated with it, we may, along with Hathaway, well wonder "why Castelvetro is talking about marvels at all."[4] Somewhat more familiar to modern eyes is the list of the sources of the marvelous offered by Patrizi, although it too is, as Hathaway says, "confused": "ignorance, fable, novelty, paradox, augmentation, departure from the usual, the extranatural, the divine, great utility, the very precise, the unexpected, and the sudden."[5]

Indeed, one of the most striking things about reading through the literature of the marvelous in the Renaissance is what is also most striking about reading through the early history of the large literature concerning miracles that begins in the classical world and carries right on through the middle ages, the Renaissance, and up to the present day.[6] As long as the discussions remain fairly general, they look quite sensible to modern eyes; but as soon as the credibility of particular events comes up, things begin to look strange indeed, and it becomes very difficult to understand why the same man who a moment before had seemed so sensible is now talking about men without heads and with eyes in their breasts. Here is Mazzoni, in a passage that clearly distances both the medieval and the Renaissance views from the modern, struggling with just this belief in Augustine:

> Now we must realize that this fiction of Homer and of Aristeas is not entirely impossible according to the ordinary course of nature, since St. Augustine tells of having seen men of this sort in lower Ethiopia. . . . And in the same place he says that he has been to preach the gospel to the Blemii, a people of interior Africa. . . . St. Augustine says this of the Blemii, that they were men without heads and that they had a single eye in their breasts. This was earlier said by Pliny in the 5th, by Pomponius Mela in the P., and by Solinus in Chapter 44; but among all these there is no writer as worthy of faith as St. Augustine is, either by the quality of person

or in terms of his asserting that he has actually dealt with and had business with these people. And truly, if this Sermon is really by that glorious saint, we must either say that this sort of man-monster has become extinct because of war or some other fortunate happening, or else, we must confess, they live in a more remote and secret part of Africa than the all-conquering armies of Philip of Austria, King of Spain and Portugal, have as yet penetrated.[7]

Aside from the half-willingness to take seriously the idea of men without heads, the startling difference between the thinking here and that of a modern is in the logic of that very first sentence, which asserts that something cannot be an impossibility "according to the ordinary course of nature, *since*" it has been testified to by as great an authority as Augustine. The ordinary course of nature, in other words, is determined by written authority. We could have no clearer example of probability as founded upon the evidence of books.

For all its many references to probabilities and marvels, Renaissance literary theory does not tell us very much that is new about the history of ideas about probability. This is because—beyond some attempts at definitions that turn out to be circular and that complicate matters by dealing with a much larger body of terms that have exfoliated out of *to eikos*—it has no explicit theory of the probable; even more than Aristotle, the Renaissance literary theorist, as well as his modern commentator, assumes that everyone knows what the probable, credible, or verisimilar are as well as what marvels and impossibilities are—again, not a wholly unreasonable assumption insofar as Aristotle's definition of probability sometimes is in effect little more than "what everyone knows to be generally the case." The task for the Renaissance theorist, rather, then becomes simply to establish and enumerate the kinds of marvels that are desirable and admissible in poetry.

In the process of making those enumerations, though, the Renaissance theorist leaves behind ample evidence that the concept of the probable is at a critical, transitional moment. Mazzoni perhaps best typifies the old concept of probability as testimony, now associated with the idea of reading the world: for him, the secret meanings of the world conveyed by the allegorist were by no means human superimpositions; rather they were there in the book of nature itself, hidden only to those who did not know how to read it; they belonged, that is, to the realm of pure truth. That kind of thinking should remind us of Paracelsus. In other writers we can see more clearly modern notions emerging. Francesco Buonamici, whose *Discorsi poetici* appear at the very end of the sixteenth century, is the most interesting of these and the one whose ideas see most clearly into the next epoch.

Against writers like Castelvetro who want to give the marvelous wide play, Buonamici inclines to an art that is highly probable. But his impulses towards what we think of as realism are by no means simple, being informed by some strikingly modern distinctions concerning literature and language. He introduces into literary discussion, first of all, an awareness that the kind of credibility we attach to literature is really very different from the kind that we attach to propositions about the real world. His audience always knows it is seeing "signs" and not the "things signified": no matter how persuasive the realist illusion, "the work of verisimilitude in the spectator can never cause him— unless he is an imbecile—to mistake the thing representing for the thing represented."[8] The thought anticipates Sidney's famous remark in the *Apology* that even a child at a play who sees a sign in great letters reading *Thebes* doesn't believe that it is actually Thebes. Practically speaking, it means for example that one need not subscribe to the kind of crudely imitative fidelity that even the proponents of the marvelous like Castelvetro applaud and that become fetishes among the neoclassicists, such as the unity of time.[9] Theoretically speaking, it is an enormously important observation that points to what we shall presently see is the central fact about literary probability: that probability as a quality of a representation (as opposed to probability statements that may be represented *within* the representation) inhabits a different logical space than that of probability statements made in and about the real world. It is a point, moreover, that becomes especially important as literature moves toward modern realism—that is, toward the novel.

The difference between the thing representing and the thing represented may seem to the twentieth-century reader almost self-evident, but of course so much writing about narrative still accepts—and for important reasons—the convention that what is represented in narrative is real, that it is still on occasion necessary to remind ourselves and our students of its truth. It can still be a shock to have fiction's fictiveness brought home, and nothing brings it home quite so well not as the reader who fails to believe, but as the reader who believes too well. A professor of my acquaintance once briefly had as a student a psychotic young man who could not distinguish events depicted in a fictional narrative from those going on in the classroom. His confusions made everyone anxious, as craziness usually does, precisely because of the *serious* blurring of the distinction between fantasy and reality. This student will return to haunt our later discussions.[10]

Buonamici also sees an important distinction between the concepts of *sign* and *similitude,* which Paracelsus, we recall, had lumped together in the same, natural family:

> There are . . . signs and similitudes. Similitudes are natural; signs depend upon our will. Being natural, similitudes do not change, nor can anyone make my image not appear in the mirror with the same delineations and colors that are in me; but the signifying of anything with one word or another resides in man's will. That a piece of taffeta or a silver eagle on a pole is flag for an army depends on us, and this is a sign. The [similitudinary] image does not exist without the existence of that of which it is an image; the sign has some separate existence, like that eagle or that taffeta, and by having existence in itself becomes a sign when it is attached to the pole.[11]

There are rich anticipations here of modern ideas, and if Buonamici's distinctions between "sign" and "thing signified" or between natural "similitude" and conventional "sign" do not quite arrive at Saussurean insights, they certainly point that way. But interestingly, Buonamici's concept of verisimilitude seems almost willfully to evade the implications of his thought and to resist the leap into that modern concept of the probable as founded upon internal evidence, or the evidence of things, and which follows from a distinction between natural and conventional signs. This failure to make the leap into the modern idea of the probable may be seen among other things in his idea that not only does credibility or verisimilitude lead to emotion in the audience, but emotion in turn enhances credibility, so that any device that produces strong emotion will enhance verisimilitude. It is seen also in the following definition:

> We believe . . . that that is verisimilar to which, on the basis of some definite detail, our mind is inclined by certain circumstances which are its consequences [i.e., of the detail] and which are common to what has been or what is true, in which there is no contradiction—not with respect to the nature of the thing, but with respect to opinion. [12]

This is a definition that tries to get far, but without much success. It says that the verisimilar is what the consequences of particular details in poetry incline us to believe. (So far so good, even if so circular.) These consequences or circumstances must look like those that attend real things (circular again: they must be similar to the truth or verisimilar). Also, they must be internally consistent. This finally begins to look like a new definition, until we come to the final qualification. Buonamici seems to be on the very edge of the distinction arrived at in the Port Royal *Logic* between external and internal evidence, but then he tells us that the judgment is to be made *not* relative to the "nature of the thing," but relative to that old standby of the authority of books, "opinion." [13]

What makes Buonamici pull back is precisely the qualitative difference between poetry and real life, or, as he sees it, the difference between poetry and history. This is of course a distinction inherited from Aristotle, where it follows from the difference between universals and particulars—a subject of extended interest to Buonamici. [14] But like most of his contemporaries, Buonamici understands that distinction rather differently than we have in our reading of the *Poetics* offered earlier. Aristotle had said that poetry was more philosophical than history because it could portray events according to necessity or probability, both of which consisted of universals. History was less philosophical because it was tied to the facts of the way things have actually happened in this imperfect world of the particular, which is filled with contingency and accident. The usual Renaissance interpretation, however (and somewhat surprisingly in view of the Renaissance fondness for the marvelous), often is kinder to history. For Francesco Robortelli, for example, the necessary and the true are the same and consist of those things that have actually happened.[15] And even a professional Aristotelian and proponent of the verisimilar like Buonamici can sometimes sound like Plato: "The poet, who is not a philosopher, and who accommodates himself to common opinion, seeks out the appearances of things and leaves essences alone."[16] Weinberg gives us the following summary of Buonamici's distinction between poetry and history:

> In nature, one action follows upon another as a necessary consequence; the actions are 'true things,' having as their cause some internal, natural necessity. Historical actions are true in the same sense; they are what 'has been.' In art, there are no true actions; instead, any stated action is a sign of a real action, and others result from it not through natural necessity, but because one action appears to lead to another in a verisimilar way.[17]

Here, as in Robortelli, history is identified with the necessary, and poetry thus becomes relegated to what is now a lesser realm, that of the verisimilar. Or we could say, perhaps more accurately and from another point of view, that a split has occurred between the verisimilar—which we have been treating as one concept among many that fall under the heading of the probable—and the probable itself.[18] The verisimilar, that is, has here become quite distinct from Aristotle's probable insofar as it has lost its identity with the universal; it has become the particular detail that has merely the appearance of truth. In either case, something in the Aristotelian association of the probable with the universal has broken up, either in a split between probability and necessity or in a split in the concept of the probable itself. In an important regard, history and poetry have changed places: now it is history alone that happens according to "some internal, natural necessity."

A significant development has occurred here—or is in the process of occurring—and it is one that helps account for the problem Buonamici finds himself up against. While literary criticism has at this point by no means abandoned Aristotle's identification of poetry with the universal, in an important sense the universal has itself been devalued: it begins to look more and more like the merely ideal, which is to say, not (as it was for Plato and Aristotle) the most real essence of things, but rather the *unreal,* the fanciful. And in this shift we can see a development that will have very important consequences for our understanding of literary probability—the emergence of the modern distinction between fact and fiction or the emergence, in other words, of the modern conceptions of history and of fiction. The project of Renaissance criticism as a whole has been seen by J. E. Spingarn as the justification of poetry in the face of the objection that poetry is fictive and therefore fundamentally false.[19] And William Nelson has traced the history of Renaissance defenses against the charge of poetry's falsity in which he focuses specifically upon the emergence of the modern distinction between fiction and fact.[20] Of course already between Plato and Aristotle there is an implicit debate on this point, but that Aristotle does not make the debate explicit itself suggests that he does not see the issues as we do. For the Greeks, the explicit question was one of truth and falsity, which are not necessarily the same things as fact and fiction. Not only does the Renaissance develop a new notion of fiction as something more than a simple falsity or lie, but also a new notion of the factual or of history as well. Where to the medieval mind the only source of matters of real fact was the Bible (and thus all other accounts of the world were more or less uncertain, more or less false), the Renaissance begins to see posited the ideal of a sort of knowledge about the world not contained in scripture that in the minds of many can aspire to certainty in effect if not always in theory. It is not surprising that, even as the theory of fiction continues to pride itself on its difference from history (as in Aristotle), it should also aspire to the new prestige of history through pretending to be history. Thus the characteristic confusion of the double claim that runs through much Renaissance theory that fiction is on the one hand something more than mere history and on the other nothing less than real history. In Buonamici's distinction between poetry and history we see the effect of the new status of the world of history and fact, here very much at the expense of probability as Aristotle understood it.

The exaltation of the real as history, so necessary to the development of literary realism, leads Buonamici to precisely the concepts Hacking regards as essential to the emergence of the modern concept of probability. Aristotle's actual world of the particular (the world of history) was imperfect and often incomprehensible because subject to the irrational causation of mere accident, while the worlds of philosophy and of poetry, less actual but more real because they were the worlds of the universal, operated predictably and rationally according to the laws of necessity and probability. Probability could not always guide us to knowledge about the actual world precisely because like necessity it belonged to the universal and was thoroughly rational. But Buonamici's actual world, as we have seen, has indeed *become* rational and has lost that sublunar quality of irrational accident that it had for Aristotle. It has therefore become the sort of world in which things may well happen according to necessity and probability, the sort of world in which it may well be profitable to look for the kinds of regularity probability leads us to expect. We have also seen that Buonamici is keenly aware of the world of fiction, in contrast, as one in which there are no true actions, but only mere signs of actions, and in a successfully crafted world of this type things happen not according to necessity but according to the skill of the fiction-maker in fashioning *apparently true* or merely verisimilar connections between events. Because Buonamici has effectively reversed the Aristotelian valuations of history and poetry (and perhaps because he is so sensitive to the illusory nature of literary representation), ironically there now is no place for the emerging new concept of probability in the realm of literature, although there is plenty of newfound room for it in the realm of history, with its natural as opposed to conventional signs. Aristotle's kind of probability, so delicately balanced in the gap between certainty and opinion, has become for *literary* purposes mere verisimilitude and looks much more like Plato's (or, for that matter, Aquinas's) probability, which is at its best mere opinion.

Thus Hacking's version of the story, to the degree that it plays down Aristotle and argues for the novelty of modern probability, is in this sense vindicated: whatever may have been the idea of the probable in ancient Greece, in the Renaissance probability was strongly associated with a kind of knowledge based on mere opinion. Moreover, even though there are in discussions of literary theory signs of the newly emerging concept of probability, that new concept is emerging not only in a space conceptually distinguished from the old (now often called verisimilitude), but practically speaking segregated as well in that it will emerge in the realm of history, the realm of the real and of natural signs, while verisimilitude is relegated to the realm of literature, the realm of humanly contrived signs and mere appearances—appearances, moreover, that never really fool anyone.

If literary theory stopped with this moment in the writings of Buonamici, in other words, we could perhaps be tempted to see the modern concept of probability and its literary (and now rather distant) cousins as going their very separate ways. And indeed a certain amount of the subsequent history of literary probability might support such a conclusion, especially if we looked for example to writing about *vraisemblance* in France in the seventeenth century. Those discussions are themselves by no means unequivocal in their understanding of their terms, but often assume the *vraisemblable* to have little real connection with the true at all. Rather they tend to formulate an elaborately artificial doctrine closely connecting probability with the most notorious and rigid neoclassical notions of decorum and the unities.[21] In fact, however, the emergence of probability is of course far from complete in a figure like Buonamici. Subsequent literary history confounds the equivocal or "separate-ways" interpretation just as the subsequent history of philosophy proves the difficulty of keeping various senses of probability apart for very long. In literary history, I shall argue, it is the modern novel which brings Aristotle's conceptual heirs back into the same family—providing in the process much amusement over their mutual fortunes, hostilities, and play—and restores literary probability to its original Aristotelian place delicately poised in the gaps between certainty and opinion, necessity and contingency, the universal and the particular, the self-evident and the merely possible, reality and appearance.

Chapter V

In the Age of the Rise of the Novel

FRANCESCO BUONAMICI's *Discorsi poetici* was published in 1597. That date brings us within ten years of the first volume of Cervantes' *Don Quixote* and thus to the very threshold of the birth of the modern novel. Of course the threshold marking the origin of the modern novel is a peculiarly wide one, effectively spanning the century and more between Cervantes and Defoe, Richardson, and Fielding. During the latter part of that time, as we have seen, the modern concept of probability was also born, or rather reborn, perhaps.

The most sustained and learned history of literary probability in the eighteenth century—learned both in literary history and the history of philosophy—is Douglas Lane Patey's account in his recent book *Probability and Literary Form: Philosophic Theory and Literary Practice in the Augustan Age,* which I have already mentioned in a couple of connections, not the least of which is its criticism of Hacking's argument.[1] The general purpose of Patey's book is to recover several of the meanings that *probability* and some associated terms had for the Augustans, a recovery that is possible only when we understand the theoretical framework within which such terms actually operated. Its thesis is that the Augustans—as well as later writers in the century—subscribed to a theory of the literary work as a hierarchic structure of probable signs. Composition was understood to be the process of constructing such a hierarchy, moving from meaning to form, and interpreting was understood to be the reciprocal process moving from form to meaning by inferring meaning from the probable sign. As Patey describes the theory (at work in one of its most articulate proponents, James Beattie):

> An example of the way signs are organized is through decorums: these are rules of natural signification (i.e., of literary probability) that guide authors in making their works consistent, and guide readers (when circumstances are "probable") in their inference from signs to underlying meaning. Literary signs in general are "probable" to the degree that they point with adequate evidence to those causes (meanings) of which they are the most likely effects.[2]

This is all perfectly consistent with what we have learned about probability thus far, for our argument has been in effect that from Aristotle to the present there has been available a complex concept of probability consisting of a number of logically related though by no means identical aspects. At particular historical moments one aspect or another is likely to be most prominent, while others may be virtually eclipsed. The aspect of probability that in the eighteenth century is uppermost, by Patey's account, is that which associates probability with signs (an association we have met already in Aristotle and in Paracelsus) as well as with evidence (an association we have met throughout the history of probability). But closely connected are other aspects familiar to us also since Aristotle, for, as Patey explains, what makes the logic whereby decorums achieve their aims a probabilistic one is that they render their narrations "consistent not only with accepted opinion, but with the ordinary pattern of nature (what happens most often)."[3]

The peculiarly Augustan contribution seems to be in the idea specifically of a *hierarchical* structure of signs and not in a new development in the logic of probability itself. For while there are a number of attempts in the eighteenth century, as later, to distinguish between literary and other sorts of probability, all of the varied senses that attach to the term *probability* and such closely related terms as *verisimilitude* in the period remain logically connected. Thus while any two writers in the eighteenth century, like any two writers in the Renaissance, may not agree on their terms, so that one writer's probability is often another's verisimilitude, for example, the general shape of the family of concepts we call *probability* remains pretty much the same.

Another way of saying this is to say that here, as much as and perhaps more than in any other period, almost all the aspects of the concept of probability remain relatively visible and lively. While there may indeed be a general tendency in the history of probability for those aspects associated with the authority of people to give way to those aspects associated with the way we apprehend the world of things themselves, in the eighteenth century, and especially among literary theorists, the whole range of aspects of the probable is readily apparent. Hacking's argument is that there is no general tendency, but rather a sharp discontinuity: the emergence of the modern notion of probability that makes possible the mathematical theory by discovering the concept of the evidence of things. Patey's book makes important and explicit criticisms of Hacking's argument by showing that in many writers before 1660 or so there was already an articulated notion of internal evidence, what Hacking calls the evidence of things. But an equally important if less explicit qualification of the Hacking thesis is apparent as well in that Patey provides a good many examples of writers after 1660 who hold to the notion of the probable as something which reflects opinion, whether of the wise (as in Aristotle) or of the mob (as in Plato). Thus, for example, a hundred years after the critical date that for Hacking marks the transition from old to new concepts of probability, we find Thomas Reid writing that "There is a much greater similitude than is commonly imagined, between the testimony of nature given by our senses, and testimony of men given by language."[4] Of course there is some comfort to be had here for proponents of the Hacking thesis, just because Reid's formulation "the testimony of nature given by our senses" gives so clear an account of what is meant by the evidence of things, but it is apparent too that the "modern" sense of probability is here refusing to separate itself out radically from older senses.

And the *most* modern sense—that is, the one the mathematical theory makes use of—is certainly evident in literary theory of the period too; indeed, it has been evident already before the eighteenth century has begun. Here for example is Dryden's striking definition of literary probability, from his 1679 Preface to *Troilus and Cressida:*

> The last quality of the action is, that it ought to be probable, as well as admirable and great. 'Tis not necessary that there should be historical truth in it, but always necessary that there should be a likeness of truth, something that is more than barely possible; *probable* being that which succeeds, or happens, oftener than it misses. To invent therefore a probability, and to make it wonderful, is the most difficult undertaking in the art of poetry; for that which is not wonderful is not great, and that which is not probable will not delight a reasonable audience.[5]

This begins as though in a straightforward Aristotelian context. It seems as though we are perhaps being offered the familiar distinction between history and poetry, but in fact we are offered a definition of probability that comes straight out of the mathematical theory—indeed, that is couched in the terms of gambling: the "*probable* being that which succeeds . . . oftener than it misses." No less significant than the definition itself is the fact that Dryden evidently sees nothing novel or inconsistent with earlier usage in it. Less than twenty years after the birth of the mathematical theory, it seems unremarkable to Dryden that mathematical and literary probability should be identically defined.

AS PATEY and others have made clear, throughout the seventeenth and eighteenth centuries the word *probability* and its paronyms and synonyms were favorites among British theorists both of poetry and of fiction.[6] To read through any neoclassical theory or to read through any of the prefaces, reviews, or early discussions of prose fiction is to encounter that family of ideas on almost every page. It is no doubt significant of an important focusing of concepts occurring in the period that terminology comes to favor the words *probability* and *probable* themselves over their synonyms, be they relatively technical (such as *verisimilitude*) or relatively ordinary (such as *likely*). Although *verisimilitude* appeared in English at the very beginning of the seventeenth century and experienced a small vogue among neoclassical critics, it is nonetheless rarely used in discussions of prose fiction in the eighteenth century and already by the end of that century has acquired for many writers a pejorative sense as having the *mere appearance* of truth.[7]

The context for reference to the probable in literary discussions was frequently an extension of Renaissance debates about marvels. And those debates of course continued with vigor beyond the sixteenth century. As Wallace Jackson says in his study of the roots of Romantic poetics, "At no time . . . was the relation between the probable and the marvelous a more lively and consistent topic of literary criticism than in the later years of the seventeenth century."[8] But important shifts of emphasis had occurred in the terms of those discussions.

One such shift is noticeable in a turning away of discussion from the explicit enumerations of marvels usual in the Renaissance. As interest in defining or representing the marvelous waned, the probable began therefore no longer to be largely referred to or defined simply by contrast with the marvelous. If the probable began to be more directly appealed to in its own right, however, this is not to say that it began to be separately defined. As had been usual since Aristotle, probability continued to be a concept that theorists generally felt was unproblematic in itself (however difficult it might be to reconcile with the marvelous) and called for no extended definition, except via the usual circular family of synonyms. Dryden's unusual definition quoted above is not really an exception in this regard. What is striking is that the definition is explicitly mathematical, but it is typical of the age in that Dryden himself evidently sees nothing remarkable or problematic in the definition.

Some implicit definitions are apparent in the formulas that attach to probability and that are already clichés by the time criticism about the novel is under way. Among the most common formulas having to do with probability in the latter half of the eighteenth century are those which refer to the "bounds of probability." Often the bounds are qualified—"narrow" is a particularly common attribute. And sometimes close synonyms are called upon—no doubt simply for variety's sake—

to suggest those bounds. Thus narratives may exceed the "limits" and "confines" of probability or a novelist may be said to transgress the "verge" of the probable. But "bounds of probability" is the favored phrase, and we find it employed by writers of all kinds. It is common in hack reviewers and can be found in more alert but still highly conventional writers—like Chesterfield—as well as in the most penetrating—like Johnson.[9] The fondness for conventional phrases and the tendency to spatialize concepts metaphorically are certainly not unexpected in a neoclassical environment, and probability is certainly not alone in being thus endowed by critics with so implicitly definite (if explicitly still undefined) a space. But that probability should be seen as fit for such spatialization tells us a good deal. The idea of "bounds" and "limits" suggests not merely spatial lines, of course, but lines beyond which one ought not in propriety to go. Probability is therefore associated with Reason, another concept that has limits and bounds, and with Rule, which denotes the original line, so to speak, or the line against which all others are measured. And indeed probability and reason are often used synonymously, probability frequently taking on attributes traditionally associated with reason. The "fantastic regions of Romance," Fanny Burney tells us in the preface to *Evelina,* are "where Fiction is coloured by all the gay tints of luxurious Imagination, where Reason is an outcast, and where the sublimity of the Marvellous, rejects all aid from sober Probability." And "the rules of probability" are appealed to by writers as different as Walpole (in the preface to the second edition of *The Castle of Otranto*) and Fielding (in the first chapter of book eight of *Tom Jones*).

These expressions would seem to return to probability a large measure of the status it had enjoyed for Aristotle insofar as probabilities were for him universals and, if what the majority of mankind believed, then at least what the majority were perfectly correct to believe. They would seem to lift probability from its medieval and Renaissance status, in which it occupied an intermediate point on the spectrum from truth to error, a point signifying not simply opinion, but opinion that may well be wrong because it is the result of mere ignorance and credulity.

No less important than this rise in dignity, moreover, is the qualita-

tive shift involved in it. For the return of probability to something
more nearly like its meaning in Aristotle at the same time entails its
emergent modern meaning. Through its association with Rule and
Reason, probability is brought back into the realm of universals, and if
probability still has the quality of opinion, it is not the opinion of the
mob, but the opinion formed by reason and good judgment. The
authority of people is giving way to the authority of things. In 1693,
René Le Bossu had written:

> I believe that the best rules for knowing how far it is permitted
> to impel the marvelous, and for knowing what will be well re-
> ceived, what will offend, and what will be ridiculed, are first
> judgment [*le bon sens*] and then the reading of good writers and even
> the examples of those who have not succeeded, comparing the one
> with the other. But in making this discrimination, one must also
> not ignore the spirit, the customs, and the manners of each century.
> For what is beautiful in Homer might have been badly received in
> the works of a poet in the time of Augustus.[10]

The authority of books holds a considerable place here, but already it is
an authority subordinate to judgment and made relative by a sophisticated understanding of the changes in belief that history brings about.
And it is an authority in a sense doubly subordinate: the authority of
books is not only to be consulted *after* judgment, but judgment is itself
employed in judging and discriminating the examples provided by
writers. Fifty years later, the authority of books of course still exerted
considerable power, but it was an authority that was being invoked, to
a much lesser extent than for Le Bossu, in the name of probability.

We have already noted one thing that demonstrates the shift: the
strengthening association between probability and reason. But perhaps
nothing demonstrates the growing separation between probability and
the authority of books so well as the other great association involving
probability in the eighteenth century, which is that connecting probability with nature. At just the time when the "bounds of probability"
are becoming a cliché, towards the middle of the eighteenth century, so
too are double references to nature and probability. They are particu-

larly frequent among the reviewers, but are common enough among the novelists themselves. Here are several examples, all written between 1750 and 1800:

Yet the Biographer [that is, the novelist] may ingraft in his Performance many Characters and Circumstances, which tho' they are entirely natural and very probable, often fall below the Dignity of the Stage.

For as the matter of them [novels] is chiefly taken from nature, from adventures, real or imaginary, but familiar, practical, and probable to be met with in the course of human life, they may serve as pilot's charts or maps of those parts of the world, which every one may chance to travel through.

The *Nouvelle Héloïse* of Rousseau is a production of a very singular kind; in many of the events which are related, improbable and unnatural; in some of the details tedious, and for some of the scenes which are described, justly blameable.

The author [Richard Cumberland], who could draw a character so utterly out of nature, and probability [as the heroine of his *Carmelite*], is likely enough to fancy that Richardson's works may be injurious to the good sense, the manners, and the morals of our youth.

We shall not forestall his [the reader's] pleasure by detailing the particulars [of *The Mysteries of Udolpho*]: but we will not hesitate to say, in general, that, within the limits of nature and probability, a story so well contrived to hold curiosity in pleasing suspence, and at the same time to agitate the soul with strong emotions of sympathetic terror, has seldom been produced.

To represent scenes of familiar life in an elegant and interesting manner, is one of the most difficult tasks an author can take in hand; for of these, every man is a critic: Nature is, in the first place, to be attended to, and probability is not to be lost sight of; but it must be nature strongly featured, and probability closely bordering on the marvellous; the one must touch upon extravagance, and the other be highly seasoned with adventures—for who will thank us for a dull and lifeless journal of insipid facts? Now every peculiarity of humour in the human character is a strain upon nature, and every surprising incident is a degree of violence to probability: how far shall we go then for our reader's amusement? how soon shall we stop in consideration of ourselves? There is undoubtedly a land-mark in the fields of fancy, *sunt certi denique fines* [there are, in short, fixed bounds], but it requires a nice discernment to find them out, and a cautious temper not to step beyond them.[11]

It is difficult in each of these examples to make any discriminations between the natural and the probable at all. Only in the second is there at least a kind of ranking, the probable (along with the "familiar" and the "practical") being presumably a kind of subhead of the natural. But there nature nonetheless is itself probabilistic—and in an unambig-uously modern sense—because the events taken from nature by novel-ists chart "those parts of the world which every one may *chance* to travel through." Obviously where the double reference is minimal—as in "the limits of nature and probability" or "improbable and unnat-ural"—there are no discriminations to be made, but even in the longer discussion in the last example, which is from book four, chapter one, of Richard Cumberland's *Henry,* one could without loss of sense inter-change the terms, so symmetrical is their use. Although nature is associated with character and probability with plot, it would hardly matter if Cumberland had written: "Now every peculiarity of humour in the human character is a strain upon probability, and every surpris-ing incident is a degree of violence to nature." And indeed in the first example nature and probability are called upon to judge both charac-ter and plot, and in the fourth example (coincidentally attacking Cumberland) both nature and probability are again called on to judge character.

The closeness of the association between nature and probability in these examples may remind us of Aristotle's twin formula, used so often in the *Poetics,* "according to necessity or probability." This formula again brings us back to the topic of universals, for we should recall that Aristotle makes use of the phrase to signify the principles that govern character and action in poetry, a realm that, unlike history, is subject to none of the distracting particulars of the contingencies that occur in the real world; poetry, rather, is subject only to the ideal and the universal, and probabilities for Aristotle of course are universals, although universals that fall just short of being necessities. The probable and the verisimilar also had retained some of the qualities of universals for the Renaissance theorist as well, insofar as they represented an *accurate likeness* to truth, as opposed to a *mere appearance* of truth. But it is, we have seen, precisely this distinction concerning the accuracy of the representation that became problematic in the course of Renaissance literary theory, where history comes to be identified in the minds of many with the real and poetry with the merely ideal, and where the modern concept of probability can be seen for a writer like Buonamici as therefore emerging in the province of history, while poetry is effectively left with the old probability and verisimilitude, which have degenerated so far as to stand for the mere appearance and form of truth.

So there is much that the early theory of probability in the novel (as it is understood in conventional references to it in the writings of quite ordinary eighteenth-century critics) has in common both with Aristotle's theory and with that of the proponent of the modern concept of probability: probability has returned to its high status among the universals and begins to look not like the mere opinion of the ignorant and credulous, but the opinion of the wise; notably, it now decidedly looks like something that emerges from the study of nature rather than the study of books.

There is ample evidence too for such shifts in the meaning of probability in less common but much more explicit references to probability as a calculus of chances. Paul K. Alkon has demonstrated Robinson Crusoe's virtual obsession with calculating odds, an obsession that is characterological and connected with one of the novel's great themes, Providence, which of course entails seeing into the future.[12] The thematization of what is unambiguously the new probability at the very beginning of the modern novel is auspicious, certainly. But a passage like the following, which occurs in an anonymous pamphlet of 1751, is suggestive of an even more deeply formal connection between the calculus of chances and the novel: "We are too well assured of *Gil Blas*'s Prosperity a long time beforehand, to be surpriz'd at it. But at the Beginning of the last Book of *Tom Jones,* the Reader is apt to think it an equal Chance whether he is to be hanged or married."[13] The doctrine of equal chances, or equipossibility, was most famously laid down by Laplace at the end of the eighteenth century, but in fact had been well-known throughout the century.[14] Whether that doctrine is specifically being referred to here is not clear, and it does not much matter, for in any case mathematical odds are explicitly if metaphorically being figured. In this example, it is not a character who is engaged in calculating probabilities, but the reader, who has been skillfully held in perfect suspense—perfect because there is no greater or lesser likelihood of either alternative occurring; the uncertainty therefore is complete.

But interesting as these examples are (and we shall look both at the thematization of probability and the reader's probabilistic uncertainty more closely later on), references to the mathematics of probability are rare in the history of the novel, for the good reason that few readers and even fewer novelists have had so much as an amateur's knowledge of the sorts of calculations involved. (Indeed, there is only one prominent figure in British literary history with any claim to expertise, and that is Dr. Arbuthnot; in 1692 he translated Huygens's classic textbook on probability and twenty years later published a paper that argued for providential design from statistical evidence about the relative frequency of male and female births.)[15] The importance for our purposes of the mathematicization of probability in any case lies not in the actual calculations made. It is rather that the mathematicization points to the fact that probability has been brought into the realm of the evidence of things, the realm of modern inductive logic and science, and the realm in which calculation becomes possible.

Perhaps an even clearer example of the new kind of evidence that was now being brought to bear in determining literary probability occurs in an exchange between Albrecht von Haller, a Swiss scientist as well as poet and writer of fiction, and Samuel Richardson. Von Haller had written a long and critical commentary on *Clarissa,* which was translated for the *Gentleman's Magazine* and appeared along with a series of footnotes offering point-by-point rebuttals, written anonymously by Richardson, who was a friend of the editor. Here is a long excerpt from that exchange:

> It is even a doubt with me [writes von Haller], whether probability is preserved in the detestable audacity of *Lovelace;* to carry a lady of quality to a brothel, to confine her a captive there against her will, to give her opium, and to violate her person. Is this possible in a country so jealous of its laws and its liberty? Can it be thought that *Lovelace,* who was not deficient in understanding, and who expected to be a peer of the realm, would expose himself to the persecution of a powerful family, exasperated against him, beyond the possibility of reconciliation? An answer to these questions can only be expected from a native of *England.*
>
> As to the improbability [Richardson replies] supposed by the ingenious and good natur'd remarker, of carrying a lady of quality to a bad house, &c. we shall leave it to the author to defend this part of his history. Mean time we may observe, from many places in the story, that this house was a place of genteel appearance; that two of the principal women in it were persons of education, ruined by *Lovelace,* and therefore entitled, as he might think, to his consideration; and who maintain'd great outward decency, especially when in the presence of *Clarissa;* who, tho' she liked them not, little imagin'd what they were. The lady was not a captive in the house. She thought herself at liberty . . . to go and come as she pleas'd. . . . [*Lovelace*] defied the laws of his country, as too many of his cast do. . . . Are there not such men in all nations? Need we refer to the public executions for crimes the most atrocious? . . .
>
> The author seems to us, to have provided against the main force of this objection of improbability, on this head, by giving early the situation of the house: A back-house within a front one; the lady

residing in the latter, as the most elegant, and most retired; the two houses communicating by a long passage, and made secure with doors within, and iron rails without, as if for ornament. A house made convenient, as *Clarissa* afterwards says, for dreadful mischief.[16]

These are not passages likely to strike modern readers as remarkable, because we have all seen countless discussions of novels that are identical in kind. But in fact they exemplify a kind of thinking that was, in so pure a form, unknown in the Renaissance and yet commonplace and normative by the middle of the eighteenth century.

What is of historic significance here is the kind of evidence being marshaled on either side. There is no trace of the old verisimilitude or probability which has credibility because it has the familiar *form* of the truth—because it looks like the kinds of propositions others have uttered. The appeal here is to the way things actually are.[17] Von Haller is of course being snide and disingenuous when he says, "An answer to these questions can only be expected from a native of *England*," but that is beside the point. His argument depends solely upon the sort of evidence we today recognize as legitimate in determining historical or retrospective probability (the probability that a certain event has already occurred rather than that it is going to occur): given the evidence of Lovelace's intelligence and his attention to his own self-interest, there is no probability that such a man would commit a crime involving several calculated stages and so certain utterly to alienate a family powerful enough to ruin his ambitions. Further (and this is the disingenuous part), given the famously law-abiding and liberty-loving spirit of the English, there is no probability that such a crime (entailing accomplices and secrecy) could be carried off in that country. Richardson's response is, at least in part, equally disingenuous (he writes under the cover of anonymity, and the characterization of von Haller as "good natur'd" is plainly sarcastic), but he completely accepts the kind of argument used. He tries to show a fallacy in von Haller's assumptions about the English by arguing that everyone knows there are monstrous men and monstrous crimes in all nations; implicitly, this argues that a low probability is not the same thing as no probability. More substantially and more to the heart of von Haller's charges, he argues that von Haller has not considered all the evidence at his disposal. The peculiar physical circumstances of the house and the particular histories of the women in charge of it (all carefully detailed in the novel), the fact that Clarissa could plausibly be deceived about the character of the house and its inhabitants, together with the fact that she did not consider herself a captive—these circumstances all give the crime some degree of probability.

The attention to circumstantial detail in these arguments may recall the Port Royal *Logic*'s discussion of "internal circumstances," which Hacking equates with the evidence of things. It should in any case certainly make us see how fully the modern concept of probability has emerged in literary discussion. (We shall later consider the fact that there is indeed something odd about the very purity of the argument here, which actually depends more exclusively on the evidence of things than would such discussions about nonfictional people and events.) The attention to circumstantial detail should be familiar also to those who know the classic account of the early modern novel in Ian Watt's *The Rise of the Novel*,[18] for it figures there as an essential and perhaps the central component of what Watt calls "formal realism": it is through the detailed descriptions of circumstantial evidence that novels are able, in this view, to present a narrative that readers will recognize as "a full and authentic report of human experience."[19] Indeed, sufficiently familiar is this technique that we may ask whether, in pointing to the circumstantiality of the exchange between Richardson and von Haller, we have not simply rediscovered the conventions of that realistic narrative technique with which we are already well familiar. In a sense that is just what we have done, although the fact that we have come at that technique via the history of the concept of probability will open up insights into the form of the novel that are not possible in the traditional account of novelistic realism as told by Watt.

It may equally be objected at this point by readers of recent literary theory that neither the exchange between von Haller and Richardson nor Watt's description of formal realism are any longer of fundamental interest. The two eighteenth-century figures make impossibly naïve arguments: they are arguments that blithely talk about characters and events in novels as though they had actual existence. Moreover, while Watt explicitly recognizes the merely conventional quality of such "realism," his account is itself full of inconsistencies and in practice he himself manages to forget the fictionality of fictions and often writes of novelistic reality as though it were real.[20] But this objection is itself naïve in supposing that one can easily dismiss the novelist's powerful urge to represent or incorporate the real world or that there is a discourse in which to talk about the novel as a realistic form that does not itself adopt the language of realism.[21] And it is naïve too in supposing that the discovery of fiction's fictionality is a recent one—recall Buonamici's point about the theater audience, who, unless they are imbecile or demented (like my colleague's student who really and frighteningly could not distinguish between what was going on in a medieval romance and what was going on in a classroom), are always perfectly aware that the people and things doing the signifying in front of them are not in fact the things signified. But of course the form of the discourse in these arguments and their failure to acknowledge the fictionality of fiction are very important. As shall become apparent later, more than our own common sense tells us that Richardson and von Haller are not taken in by the fiction, but in order better to understand the significance of fiction's blindness to itself as well as to see how coming at the origins of the modern novel via the history of the concept of probability alters a traditional description of the novel's realism, it will be helpful to ask more fundamental questions about the nature of literary probability than I have done to this point. Such will be the task of the following chapter.

THUS FAR we have looked at the philosophical history of probability and at its manifestations of literary history. We have seen that in spite of apparent ambiguity or equivocality, the range of senses of probabil-

ity has enough coherence for us to talk about *the* concept of probability
from Aristotle to the present and have some assurance that the probability of the scientist and of the poet are therefore not fundamentally
different in kind. We have seen that virtually the full range of senses
of this extraordinarily slippery concept is at least implicit already in
Aristotle and that the subsequent history of the concept has in a sense
involved the articulating of implications and difficulties already present
in his accounts. But we have seen, in part following and in part dis-
senting from Ian Hacking, that during the Middle Ages and Renaissance probability loses some of the senses it has for Aristotle and comes
to mean something founded largely upon the evidence of people and
that it is only late in the seventeenth century that the concept as entailing something founded upon the evidence of things fully emerges—
or reemerges. We have seen also that literary references to probability
are generally consistent with this emerging concept and that by the
middle of the eighteenth century there are discussions of literary probability that depend *exclusively* upon the evidence of things—that belong
fully to modern senses of probability associated with the mathematical
theory of probability. But what remains to be done is to explain what
the special consequences of the emergence of modern probability are
for literature, beyond showing that they lead to a technique that looks a
lot like realism as it is traditionally described. For the consequences of a
realist discourse founded upon probability are very considerable: such
a discourse conceals not only the fictionality of fiction but an important
oddity that comes into play whenever one talks about probability in
connection with fictions at all. It derives from the central and definitive
fact that fictions are made-up stories, a fact that has been made much
of in the history of discussions of fictions; but it is an oddity that nevertheless goes unremarked in all the literary discussions of *probability* that
I know, from Aristotle's on, and one that I too have left unremarked
until now.

Chapter VI

The Antinomy of Fictional Probability

WHEN ARISTOTLE moves from a general discussion of probability to a discussion of it in relation to literature, he never pauses to say that there is something peculiar in the logic of literary probability. On the contrary, the probability of literature is for him identical to the probability in any kind of discourse: it is a standard against which we measure literature, just as it is a standard against which we measure, for example, the testimony of a witness in court or a prediction about tomorrow's weather. There are obscurities in the concept, to be sure, and I have earlier called probabilities "ghostly things." This ghostliness has to do with the fact that probabilities seem precariously poised between the universal and the particular, the certain and the contingent: they are like signs that point to truths, but they are more than signs, because signs are particulars one may observe while probabilities are universal propositions, and in that sense therefore unobservable in themselves, rather like innate ideas. Aristotle's probabilities inhabit the gap in logic that later became known as "the problem of induction." But these obscurities affect probabilities in all realms. If *to eikos* is "the likely" or "like truth," then we should be able to say that probability provides a standard against which one can measure the accuracy of testimony or the accuracy of a fictional imitation—difficult though it may be to define exactly what that standard is.

Nor do Aristotle's successors define a special logical space for the operation of fictional probability—certainly neither the neoclassicists, for whom probability is associated very clearly with rule and with reason, nor even so self-conscious a critic as Buonamici, who is fully aware that the signs of a fictional representation do not point to actual truths at all. For him as for Aristotle, probability remains a standard against which to measure fictional imitations; in his case, and because the signs are not in fact the things signified, the standard entails the mere, illusory, appearance of truth.

In the eighteenth century we do indeed see a vocabulary that suggests a distinction between literary or poetic and ordinary probability, but rather than distinguishing between the sort of probability we make use of in thinking about fictions from that we make use of in thinking about the real world, this turns out to mark a distinction between two sorts of standard of probability, *both* of which are made use of in fictions—poetic probability sometimes meaning inner consistency and sometimes fidelity to psychological truth (poetic probability thus having as its object a special sort of poetic truth), while ordinary probability is reserved for fidelity to the facts of the real world, usually facts of the most familiar sort (ordinary probability thus being associated with the development of realism).[1]

If we inquire into what is meant by using probability as a standard against which to judge fictions, however, we encounter problems, and there turns out to be something at best empty, at worst circular about applying such ghostly standards. Consider Aristotle's example of a probability: "the envious hate." What would it mean to measure a novel against it? Perhaps a certain novel's plot leads us to such a generalization: that is, the novel is full of envious people, and they hate. Then we can say that against the standard of a certain probability this novel passes the test of probability, its characters are probable. But of course too, as Aristotle tells us, it is probable that improbabilities will happen. The envious do not *always* hate; indeed, if they did always hate then "the envious hate" would be a necessity rather than a probability. Perhaps in the novel there are some envious who do not hate; is their existence a violation of probability? It all depends, of course, upon their particular circumstances, and becomes a question of evidence.

In fact it is a maxim of modern probability theory that probability is always relative to evidence. Something, say my uncle's owning a motorcycle, does not have probability *in itself,* but only relative to the evidence we have that is relevant to his case. If I have statistical tables concerning the ownership of motorcycles that break down the population of owners into categories which are pertinent to things I know about my uncle—age, address, marital status, income, other consumer goods owned and so on—then I can calculate a mathematical probability of motorcycle ownership for the set of men to which my uncle belongs, and make my bets accordingly.[2] But I can also determine the probability based upon other kinds of evidence too, of course—what the neighbors say, a receipt from a motorcycle service center, even my uncle's own word for it (and taking into account what I know about the value of that). But in actual fact he either owns a motorcycle or does not, and it makes sense to ascribe a probability to that ownership only when I have no certain knowledge of that fact and relative to the evidence of the incomplete knowledge I do have.

How does probability's being relative to evidence affect fictional probability? Reconsider the exchange about Lovelace between von Haller and Richardson, which we saw was based upon precisely the kind of evidence today regarded as valid: von Haller drew evidence from the real world, and Richardson responded with evidence from the novel; the evidence of the real world functions to determine the probabilities associated with the set of young men to which Lovelace belongs—it determines the standard of probability against which the novel is measured—while Richardson's evidence particularizes the individual case and so defines precisely which set Lovelace belongs to. Now in such an exchange the evidence of the novel has an unbeatable advantage. We know how such arguments always continue and end. More objections based upon the tendency of people in the real world to behave in certain ways will be countered by appeals to more evidence in the novel that explains these special circumstances. Evidence from the novel of course is undeniable (except when it is carefully —that is, in carefully circumscribed ways—rendered doubtful by an unreliable narrator), and, as it accumulates, the set of real young men that determines the probability of Lovelace's behavior becomes ever smaller as detail upon detail about the fictional Lovelace is added.

Rather eerily, the "probabilities" to which appeal is made begin to assume more and more the shape of the fiction in question. Mirror-like, they mimic whatever they are asked to judge. Inevitably the set of "real" young men becomes a set with only one member and the question ultimately posed is the circular one: How probable is it that a young man exactly like Lovelace would behave exactly like Lovelace? Presumably von Haller would see his logical fate before he came to this point, but at some point he would have to throw up his hands and say, "I don't care about all that. I don't believe in Lovelace anyway." This is an effective way out, in a sense, because there is no argument against disbelief, no argument that can compel belief. Having withheld belief from Lovelace, von Haller would then be in a position to do what he has wanted to do all along: rewrite the novel. To disbelieve, however, is to discount any of the evidence the novel does provide but that one chooses to discount, and in that case there can be no meaningful discussion of probability either.

But perhaps the oddity arises only because we have construed the question somewhat perversely. If the question really is, How probable is it that a young man exactly like Lovelace would behave exactly like Lovelace? then certainly something is very odd indeed about questions of literary probability. But surely real readers don't pose such strange questions. Suppose instead we construe the question as, How probable is it that someone behaving as Lovelace does—taking at least a central core of his qualities—might exist in the real world? Is not this a more reasonable way to ask the question, and can't we with confidence say that Lovelace is on this basis a far more probable character than, say, Superman? Viewed in this way, the problem of fiction becomes something very like the problem of counterfactuals: If Lovelace were real—again taking at least a central core of his qualities—would he behave just as the novel has him behave? Such is in fact the theory of fiction proposed by David Lewis.[3] But these apparently reasonable ways of posing the question have slipped something crucial by us. Who is to say what constitutes "a central core of his qualities"? His qualities can be known only through what we know of his behavior —through, that is, the evidence that the novel presents us with. The conventions of fiction surely require us to accept that evidence; we are not free arbitrarily to accept some details of a text and reject others. If we accept what we are told about Lovelace, then a "central core of his qualities" would have to be consistent with *everything* we know of him. And we could develop an idea of that core only by treating the character as real, thus begging the question of his probability, for if we *do* accept the evidence of the text entirely then it makes no sense to raise the question of probabilities. Only by choosing to doubt some feature of Lovelace as the text presents him do we create a logical space in which probabilistic inference can operate, but to do that we have to jump outside the fictional world and its conventions.

Another objection to the oddity might be that it arises only when we make use of the wrong aspect of probability. If we are thinking about that aspect of probability that governs belief, its subjective or epistemological side, then it is indeed logically odd to ascribe probabilities to events whose occurrence (or nonoccurrence) we are already certain of. But suppose questions of fictional probability are really questions about the objective aspect of probability, the sort of absolute probability that a die has of turning up a three and that is entirely separate from my knowledge or beliefs? In this sense might it not be perfectly reasonable to say that such and such a character or event has a high or low degree of probability quite independent of its actual existence, just as it is perfectly reasonable to say that the best market research ascribes a probability of .015 to my uncle's owning a motorcycle (even though I know for a fact he has three of them)? It may in this sense be reasonable, but also beside the point. That I have a probability of living until I am seventy is quite meaningless if my body is riddled with cancer. That my die has a probability of turning up three of 0.1666666666666 is meaningless if I have just failed to turn up a three in a dozen throws. Such absolute or objective probabilities are abstractions that attach only to other abstractions: hypothetical sets of people who really do all die at age 70.04327 or a hypothetical perfectly balanced die that imaginarily turns up threes precisely one time in six. Precisely because it is probable that improbabilities will happen, they are of use only in making bets about large populations and events that occur in the long run; they are of no use in making bets about individuals or about events in the short run. Thus while fictional characters may reasonably be said to possess such probabilities, such probabilities cannot be invoked to avoid the sort of probabilistic argument about the circumstances of individuals in which von Haller and Richardson find themselves. As in the case of the last objection, we can attach some degree of probability to Lovelace only by reference to some statistical set to which he belongs. But which facts about him do we include in defining the set and which do we exclude? A reader sympathetic to his "probability" can always object to *whatever* details from the text we exclude and so force us to define the set finally as the set that is occupied solely by a person exactly like Lovelace. And that move returns us to the form in which we originally asked the question: How probable is it that a young man exactly like Lovelace would behave exactly like Lovelace? In other words, to the extent that we can separate epistemic and objective senses of probability, the latter turn out to be uninteresting to readers like von Haller and Richardson, who, of course, really are after all interested in questions of credibility rather than in placing bets.[4]

To regard probability as providing a standard against which fictions may be measured, therefore, creates an absurd situation, like talking about the probability of my uncle's owning a motorcycle when I know full well that he does own one. To accept the conventions of realism is self-evidently to accept the matter of fictions as real, and one cannot doubt their probability except by jumping out of the conventions. If the probable is that which is verisimilar, "like the truth," then necessarily the matter of fictions *is* probable when one accepts the convention of reading them as true.[5] And the problem does not go away if we take the other fundamental—and logically prior—meaning of probability, which is closer to "like *to be* true." For what is central to the semantic function of *probability* is the ability to assert something about past, present, or future in spite of less than complete knowledge about that thing: probability statements function in nondemonstrative arguments about matters of fact. That attribute has defined the logical space of probability from before Aristotle. But literary fictions do not make such arguments of fact. They only pretend to make statements about reality—again, as everyone not mad or imbecile knows. As we shall later see, it is only the fact of pretense that makes probabilistic statements about fictions make any sense at all.

This logical strangeness follows from fiction's essential fictionality and is therefore necessarily connected with it. But while we are in some sense simply rediscovering the fictionality of fiction when we come upon the strangeness from the perspective of probability, it is important that we do so, for discussions of probability veil fictionality in a way that discussions of the reality in fictions do not.[6] A discussion that begins to look as if it takes the *actual* existence of a fictional character seriously will quickly be recognized even by the most naïve as imbecile or mad; but even though the heyday of literary probability has long passed, it is not uncommon to hear sophisticated critics make at least informal invocations of probability. Why that should be—why the concept of probability still finds a use in criticism in spite of its logical strangeness in discussions of fiction—is therefore one of the large questions this study inquires into. If the answer accords probability some degree of respectability, then something important about realist claims will have been reaffirmed.

To sum up: Probability statements about the characters or plots in imaginative literature logically belong to a different space than do statements about the real world, and there is something fundamentally strange—or absurd—about discussions of the probability of Mr. Pickwick, say. Why should there ever be a question about the "probability" of people and events that are known certainly never to have existed or occurred? This logical strangeness is in fact the distinguishing feature of questions about what is probable in literature and therefore important enough to be marked by its own name. I call it the antinomy of fictional probability.[7]

A commonsensical answer to the question of why one talks about the probability of Lovelace of Mr. Pickwick is that the conventions of realism demand that we treat fictions as real, and treating something as real (or as a matter of fact) necessarily allows us to entertain probabilistic arguments about it. This answer further means that talk about the probability of character and plot is simply the sign that fiction is an imitation of the real, and the antinomy occurs only when one jumps outside the conventions, from the representation to the real world, and then looks back across the gap. This jump is like the jump from one universe to another, because it involves changing an entire set of assumptions about reality and the withholding of belief from a world in which one has just been absorbed. That the literary probable is the sign of literary imitation is as much as to say that whenever the question of probability in literature is raised, what really is being discussed is the credibility of the imitation. (One school of theoreticians of probability, remember, says that probability is the measure of our belief in an assertion.)

Intuitively, this answer may seem to have a good deal to recommend it. But before examining the merits of the argument, note that some of the "common sense" here first of all is itself quite advanced in its understanding: it recognizes something called the conventions of realism—implying that these conventions are arbitrary, not natural —and is able to jump in and out of their discourse, presumably at will. This is certainly not the common sense of ancient Greece, nor of the Renaissance, for it all too easily discloses what both Aristotle and the typical Renaissance theorist were at pains either to conceal or to justify: that fictions utter falsehoods. Nor is it eighteenth-century common sense, surely, for even if eighteenth-century novelists and critics are not taken in by the illusion, they certainly are taken in by the discourse: they believe in the *accuracy* of the imitation; nowhere do we find the kind of conceptual agility that characterizes our "commonsensical" answer and nowhere do we find acknowledgement of the antinomy.

If in practice eighteenth-century critics move between the discourse that operates under the conventions of realism and the discourse that recognizes the fictionality of fiction, the moves are un-self-conscious and the gap goes unremarked. Consider the following sentence from a review of Charlotte Smith's *The Old Manor House:* "Several of the less important characters, both in high and low life, are equally well drawn [as the major ones]; and the piece, on the whole, is a gallery of portraits, of which it would not be difficult to find the originals in real life."[8] Such references to the accuracy of character-drawing are almost as common in the latter half of the eighteenth century as formulas about the "bounds of probability." And to modern readers the nonsensicality of talking about the accuracy of portraits of people who never lived is self-evident.

But perhaps we are being unfair to the understanding of our eighteenth-century writer. The apparent absurdity of such comments as the above is explained when we understand that they leave out a necessary assumption about just what it is that fiction is accurate in relation to. In the preface to *Evelina,* Fanny Burney makes that assumption explicit:

> To draw characters from nature, though not from life, and to mark the manners of the times, is the attempted plan of the following letters. . . . The heroine of these memoirs, young, artless, and inexperienced, is
>
> No faultless Monster, that the world ne'er saw,
>
> but the offspring of Nature, and of Nature in her simplest attire.

The distinction between nature and life, a descendant of the distinction between universals and particulars, provides the apparent way out of the absurdity. Burney is subscribing to good Aristotelian and Augustan practice: accuracy means accuracy to the truth of nature, not accuracy to the particulars of real life, and no pretense about the "reality" of Evelina is in fact being made. But the appeal to nature does not resolve the problem. Remember the formula "nature and probability" and its Aristotelian ancestor, "necessity or probability." The appeal to nature is an appeal once again to a probabilistic standard against which to judge the novel. (In fact the ellipsis in the quotation just cited contains the invocation to "sober Probability" cited earlier.) And we have seen how that appeal to the standard of probability leads inevitably to the antinomy.

In practice it proves impossible to maintain the fiction that no fiction is being maintained. In the very moment that the universality or idealness of Evelina is being asserted, Burney asserts just the opposite. Evelina is not nature in herself, but "the *offspring* of Nature"—

moreover, the offspring of "Nature in her *simplest* attire," which apparently means the most ordinary and familiar attire, that which is most easily recognized from experience of the real world. And, what is most plainly contradictory to Burney's claim that she is drawn from nature, not life, she is said to be "no faultless Monster, that the world ne'er saw," which is actually to say she is no ideal character at all, but what the real world has in fact seen.

Here is another eighteenth-century writer, James Beattie in his essay of 1783 "On Fable and Romance," stumbling less gracefully over the same problem:

> The love of Truth is natural to man; and adherence to it, his indispensable duty. But to frame a fabulous narrative, for the purpose of instruction or of harmless amusement, is no breach of veracity, unless one were to obtrude it on the world for truth. The fabulist and the novel-writer deceive nobody; because, though they study to make their inventions probable, they do not even pretend that they are true: at least, what they may pretend in this way is considered only as words of course, to which nobody pays any regard.[9]

This begins well enough with its promise to reconcile fiction and truth and its well-taken point—virtually the same we have seen Buonamici and Sidney make—that nobody is actually fooled by a pretense of fictions to literal truthfulness. The stumbling occurs when Beattie argues that nobody is deceived because there are no attempts to deceive and no such pretensions anyway, for as he immediately after recognizes, there are of course such pretensions. Perhaps he has mainly in mind such protestations of authenticity as Defoe makes in his prefaces to *Robinson Crusoe* and *Moll Flanders*. But without the conventional realist technique of writing *on every page* as though about matters of fact, there would be no fiction at all. To dismiss these pretensions merely as "words . . . to which nobody pays any regard" is plainly lame, but it is more than that: it is to deny fiction's formal essence.

Because of its commitment to the discourse of the *accuracy* of realism, therefore, eighteenth-century literary criticism does not possess the same "common sense" available to us and therefore cannot generate our "commonsensical" answer to the question of why one talks about the probability of character or plot in the novel. But different as eighteenth-century discourse is, our more complex and powerful "commonsensical" answer is itself mistaken. Let us recapitulate that answer and consider its merits.

The "commonsensical" answer says most simply that novels and other fictions require us to talk about fictional things *as though* they were matters of fact and that treating things *as* matters of fact opens up the possibility of making probabilistic arguments about them. And it attaches an explanation to that answer: one becomes aware of the antinomy only when one *stops* treating the matter of fiction as matter of fact and in so doing jumps outside novelistic convention. This is like jumping between universes, and to be able to jump from the fictional universe to the universe of the real world is to be able to look back and see the antinomy of fictional probability as the gap between them. What discussions of fictional probability amount to, then, are discussions simply of credibility, and to ascribe probability to fictional matter is to assert its believability.

There are several errors here. The first has to do with the answer as most simply put: while it is true that the conventions of realism allow us at least formally to make probabilistic propositions about the matter of novels—because that matter is presented as matter of fact—it overlooks a point that by now should be second nature in supposing that readers stop with a consideration merely of the form of propositions. Actual readers test their truth as well—with the familiar exceptions of imbeciles and the insane; when Raskolnikov kills the old lady, we do not—fortunately—call the cops. And in this truth-testing itself, the jump and the antinomy appear.

The first error explains the second, which comes in supposing that the jump occurs relatively rarely. For to say that the antinomy isn't very important because one is aware of it *only* when the jump occurs is to suggest that the jumps are rare in fact and perhaps not inevitable at all—occurring, say, when one puts the novel in which one has been absorbed down and subsequently self-consciously reflects upon it as a fiction.[10] But if the jump isn't necessary then one is on the one hand imbecile or mad or on the other hand wholly incapable of assenting to the conventions not only of realism, but of any kind of storytelling at all; it may easily be doubted that the latter sort of creature has ever existed. If the jump *is* necessary, but occurs at long intervals, then the reader is a perhaps stranger creature still who behaves like a fool or madman half the time and like the sternest rationalist or positivist the rest of the time. None of these readers is very plausible, of course.

The third error lies in supposing that the problem of probability can be simply and completely reduced to one of belief, and in part this error also is a descendant of the first. For to talk about the reader's belief in a fiction is again to suppose something that manifestly is untrue: if we are to talk about belief in fiction, it must be belief of a highly qualified and complex kind. So to "reduce" the problem of probability to one of belief is no reduction at all; it is as inadequate—and circular—as defining the probable as the likely or the verisimilar.

Neither eighteenth- nor twentieth-century common sense, then, is satisfactory in explaining how it is that we can talk reasonably about the probability of novels whenever we inquire into the logic of fictional probability. Of course, nothing compels us to explore that logic. When Douglas Patey or any other intellectual historian wants to explore the question of what probability meant to literary theorists in the eighteenth century, it is quite possible to do so without coming up against the antinomy, for all we have to do to avoid the antinomy is to overlook or take for granted fiction's fictionality by being silent and un-self-conscious about our multiple crossings in and out of fictional worlds. At one moment we write about fictions as if they asserted things about the real world; at another we write as though they are mere constructs without real reference. And this is of course what literary critics and theorists do all the time. In the next section we shall discuss the good reasons for this. But if we do choose to explore that prior logic of fictionality, and if, like Aristotle, like Patey, and, like many of the modern philosophers of probability, we take seriously a fundamental kinship in the senses of *probability,* then we come hard up against an antinomy whenever we inquire into the logic of fictional probability. If we do *not* take that kinship seriously, then there is a major gap between what Aristotle has to say about probability in the *Prior Analytics* and *Rhetoric* and what he has to say about it in the *Poetics*.

This is an unattractive dilemma, and there is no simple way out, but there is at least a way to describe the relation between probability and fictions that does not leave us at the impasse of the antinomy. Philosophy cannot provide much direct help here, because philosophers have not paid much notice to literary discussions of probability. But in the context of ordinary language and in a context not far removed from the literary, they have occasionally come upon something that looks a lot like the antinomy of literary probability. I mean the kind of expressions that once upon a time enticed us to read newspaper columns about oddities or to visit sideshows—expressions like "improbable but true."

A number of philosophers have worried about whether such expressions are solecisms, and usually the answer has been yes.[11] Max Black suggests why when he offers a logical equivalent. "There is an absurdity," he writes, "in saying 'Probably a black ball will be drawn [out of a bag that holds black and white balls], but all the same a black ball will not be drawn.'"[12] To ascribe probability to a proposition is in Black's view as well as in Toulmin's to give qualified assent to it, and it is absurd simultaneously to assent to a proposition and to deny it. As Toulmin says, "No one person is permitted, in one and the same breath, to call the same thing both improbable and true . . . : to do this is to take away with one hand what is given with the other."[13] Hacking quotes a footnote in Gibbon's *Decline and Fall* which exhibits the same difficulty. Gibbon had said of an event, "Such a fact is probable but undoubtedly false," and Hacking uses that utterance to point to the dead and (to modern eyes) very peculiar senses of probability that are connected with approbation and are the heirs to Aquinas's *opinio*.[14] If probability has to do with knowledge that is uncertain, how can it be an attribute of something that is in fact certainly known?

I suspect that most readers of the present study will immediately feel the absurdity of Black's proposition about drawing from a bag balls that probably will be black but certainly will not be. And I suspect most will also quickly see the problem with "improbable but true," even if that is a locution we are all familiar with. But I suspect further that readers familiar with the *Poetics* or with eighteenth-century literary discourse will have a harder time finding fault with Gibbon's sentence, which is not difficult to give good Aristotelian form in a paraphrase: "Such a fact occurs according to probability or is consonant with what probability would lead us to expect, but in this particular case things certainly did not in fact happen in this way. Just as it is probable that improbabilities will sometimes occur, it is probable that probabilities will sometimes not occur." The paraphrase would likely render the sentence more acceptable to most philosophers, but they would surely note that an important ellipsis has been filled in and that it is still not entirely well expressed; for what the paraphrase makes clear is that *two separate frames of reference* are at once being implicitly considered and with them *two separate bodies of evidence.* What distinguishes these examples is in fact the extent to which they imply such separate frames of reference.

The example about drawing balls out of a bag is an incorrigible absurdity because there is only one imaginable frame of reference for it, that of a person anticipating what the color of the next ball drawn will be; the evidence available in that case cannot lead both to the conclusion that a black ball will be drawn and that a black ball will not be drawn. The expression "improbable but true" might be applied to such a situation, which helps us to see it as nonsensical ("It is improbable but true that the next ball drawn will be white"). But a more usual context for the expression is, as Toulmin himself suggests, a newspaper column like "Ripley's Believe It or Not." And in such a place there are always two frames of reference being appealed to, that of common knowledge, sense, or expectation on the one hand, and that of particular experience or knowledge on the other. So the expression "improbable but true" in such a context is shorthand for, "Given what I know about the world, I would not have predicted X, but now I see (or at least believe) that X is the case." Perhaps because Gibbon's remark is plainly about something that has already happened (or not happened, actually), it is very easy to assume two frames of reference for it: it seems to invite comparison of what one might in general expect with what the good evidence about the occurrence in fact leads us to believe. (Thus the sentence "It *was* improbable that a black ball *would be* drawn, but certainly a black ball *was* drawn" does not create the same problems as, "Probably a white ball *will* be drawn, but certainly it *won't*.")

What the commonness of expressions such as "improbable but true" suggests is that under some circumstances people ordinarily do not have trouble weighing multiple frames of reference simultaneously. Because it is concise to the point of being elliptical, what looks to the philosopher like the sign of solecism and confusion may more positively look to us like the sign of an ability or faculty. This is because all of the references to literary probability we have discussed are the logical equivalents of expressions like "improbable but true" (or "improbable but false" or "probable though false" and so on): they all make ascriptions of probability in spite of certain knowledge. Either we can resign ourselves to the ill-expressedness of literary discourse or try to see if in this case, to borrow from Wittgenstein, ordinary language is not all right after all. If indeed there is an acceptable way beyond the antinomy of literary probability, it will be via the assumption of multiple frames of reference and the reader's ability to maintain such multiple perspectives—in effect simultaneously. And upon the assumption of that ability we may hope to found a more satisfying theory of literary probability, one that does not do away with the antinomy but at least gives it a manageable shape.

Part Three

A Theory of Fictional Probability

Chapter VII

Fictional Belief

PROJECTING one likely conclusion to the debate between von Haller and Richardson in the last section, we saw that it is apparently possible to evade the problem of fictional probability by reducing it to a question of belief. But we also saw that such a reduction offers no real way out at all; rather, it at best begs the question. All questions of probability necessarily depend upon questions of belief, and whenever we ask of such and such a thing, Is it probable? we are implicitly asking whether it is worthy of our belief. One of the simplest ways of pointing out the antinomy of fictional probability is in fact to notice that we do not in any ordinary sense "believe" in fictions. Precisely because in watching a play we do *not* mistake the sign "Thebes" for the city itself, it is logically strange for us to ponder probabilities in connection with a fictional "Thebes." At the same time, however, we are apt to feel there is something illegitimate in a reader's throwing up his hands (as we imagined von Haller doing) and saying, "I don't care; I don't believe in that character (or that action, or that sign) anyway." Such a reader simply turns his back on the text and thereby takes himself out of the game of criticism.

Clearly there is not only as much of a problem about the nature of our belief in fictions as there is about the probability of fictions, but the problems are in some essential way connected. Perhaps they are really the same question. In order to understand what it means that we find fictions probable or not, we must therefore understand something about the nature of our belief in fictions. And that raises a fundamental question about the nature of fiction itself, for it is of course definitive of fictions that they are about things known not to be true—again, not worthy of our belief in any ordinary sense.

From one point of view, a vast amount of literary criticism and theory is about the problem of fictional belief. Whenever writers *worry* about fiction's having as its objects things not true, then necessarily fictional belief is in question. Thus one could say that the master theme of literary theory from Plato through most of the eighteenth century is the defense of literature's fictionality and the exploration of what makes for fictional belief. But a comparatively tiny amount has been written about what we might call the logic of fictional belief just as a comparatively tiny amount has been written about the logic of fictions. As in the case of literary probability, discussions tend to assume that the concepts in question are themselves well understood and that what is of interest is *what makes for* literary belief rather than what such "belief" might fundamentally *be* or *that* we talk about literary "belief" at all —given again that we don't in fact believe in fictions in any ordinary sense.

With the important and famous exception of Coleridge, the worry about fiction for most of the history of literary criticism has been a moral rather than a logical (or psychological) one: What is the moral effect upon us of our being entertained by representations of things that never happened? With the invention of the category of the aesthetic, that worry recedes and is relegated to people largely outside the ranks of the literary. In the seventeenth and early eighteenth centuries it is common for British writers of fictions to share the worry; in the nineteenth, the worry is common only among Evangelicals and some Utilitarians not themselves involved in the literary world. With the ascendancy at the same time of realism, that worry also begins to recede, for because realism seeks an accurate representation of the world as it really is, it is of the nature of realism that it veils the fictionality of fictions: fictions whose fictionality is plain are bad fictions. Thus critics skeptical of the merely aesthetic and very much concerned with the moral effects of literature in the nineteenth and twentieth centuries—critics like Matthew Arnold and F. R. Leavis, for example—

never worry about fictions *as* fictions, but only worry about whether particular fictions see things as they really are.

As the dubiousness of the categories of the aesthetic (as independent of history and ideology, for example) and the realistic (as offering an accurate representation of reality) have become apparent to twentieth-century literary theorists and critics, questions about the logic of fictions and belief in fictions have begun to be asked frequently and from a variety of viewpoints. These have been broadly motivated by concerns with the ideological import of literature, with the phenomenology and psychology of reading, and with the philosophical status of representations.

Questions about the logic of fictions and the status of belief in fictions are necessarily philosophical ones, and fortunately there is quite a full tradition of philosophical concern about fictions, though initially this concern was not much interested in fictions as *literary* devices. Philosophers care about fictions for a number of reasons. There is considerable interest for the logician in the questions of what kind of logical sense and what kind of truth value can be assigned to statements that seem to be about fictional beings. It is important for logicians of varying kinds as well as some philosophers of science to know if fictional entities can truly be said to "exist." But among philosophers, *fictional* has usually meant "things known not to exist in the real world," and (with the leading exception of Nelson Goodman) their interest until fairly recently hasn't extended to artistic creations in ways those of us primarily concerned with art could find much sympathy with. While Mr. Pickwick was for a long time a favorite philosophical example of a fictional entity (thanks in part to his own invention of the "Pickwickian sense," which itself creates fictions), it was not really a novelistic Mr. Pickwick that philosophers were concerned with.

The situation has changed somewhat in recent years, and we can profitably look at some recent philosophical writing about fiction in some detail. A good place to begin is with the problem that fictional discourse as it occurs in works of art has been seen to pose for the proponents of J. L. Austin's speech-act theory, an outgrowth of or-dinary-language philosophy. The theory holds that communicating in language is achieved through the performance of speech acts which not only convey meaning in the usual sense, but also, in the words of Austin, "have a certain . . . force":[1] they seek to do things such as informing, warning, persuading, and so on. In fictions, however, there is a disruption between sense and the force that usually attaches to that sense; in reading novels or watching plays we do not respond to their respective speech-acts in the usual ways. As we have noted before, when we read a sign that says "Thebes" we do not take that as a cue to get out our guide to the restaurants of the city, and when we read that Raskolnikov has killed the old lady, we do not call the cops. Austin himself recognized this disruption in noting that an "utterance will . . . be in a peculiar way hollow or void if said by an actor on the stage, or if introduced in a poem," but he simply put such nonserious uses of language aside as "parasitic" upon ordinary discourse.[2]

The importance of this peculiar hollowness has been recognized by John Searle, the most important elaborator of the theory today, who addressed it in a 1975 essay called "The Logical Status of Fictional Discourse."[3] But Searle endorses Austin's questionable characterization of fictional discourse's relation to "serious" discourse as "parasitic." That characterization and Searle's endorsement of it are critically discussed by Jacques Derrida in his essays "Signature Event Context" and *"Limited Inc."*[4] His analysis entails an important deconstruction of the opposition between fact and fiction that we shall return to later on.

Recognizing a problem and solving it are two different things, and Searle's solution strikes me neither as especially original nor satisfying, though in fairness to Searle perhaps it doesn't seem so to him either.[5] It is that rather than performing actual illocutionary acts or really making assertions, works of fiction *pretend* to perform such acts, although not in the sense of having any intent actually to deceive anyone. Searle writes:

> Now *pretend* is an intentional verb: that is, it is one of those verbs which contain the concept of intention built into it. One cannot truly be said to have pretended to do something unless one intended to pretend to do it. So our first conclusion leads immediately to

our second conclusion: the identifying criterion for whether or not a text is a work of fiction must of necessity lie in the illucutionary intentions of the author. There is no textual property, syntactical or semantic, that will identify a text as a work of fiction. What makes it a work of fiction is, so to speak, the illocutionary stance that the author takes toward it, and that stance is a matter of the complex illocutionary intentions that the author has when he writes or otherwise composes it.[6]

What makes it possible for there to be fictions, which possibility for Searle is "an odd, peculiar, and amazing fact about language,"[7] is that "there are a set of conventions which suspend the normal operation of the rules relating illocutionary acts and the world." These conventions make the relaying of fictions "a separate language game," which is "not on all fours with illocutionary language games, but is parasitic on them."[8]

Now as useful as speech-act theory has lately proven to be for literary critics and theorists, I do not think that Searle has made a deep contribution to our understanding of fiction in this—not because he relies on the concept of pretending, but because he doesn't tell us much about what pretending really is and because he may be seen in any case as *misplacing* that concept. But more of that after we look at more obvious problems.

Searle appears to be confused about the question of whether or not making fictions is a "language game" at all. When he writes that "there is no textual property . . . that will identify a text as a work of fiction," he is necessarily implying that what makes fiction fiction isn't a property of language at all, and when he writes that the fictionality of a text depends upon its author's intentions, he is making the extralinguistic quality of fictions explicit. How then can it be "an odd, peculiar, and amazing fact *about language* that it allows the possibility of fiction at all"? The facts in Searle's account have to do with human intentions and human nature, not anything in the nature of language itself. If it is true that we have to look beyond language and textual properties into the realm of intentions, further, it isn't clear how then fiction-making is a "separate *language* game" that is "parasitic" upon them. If, on the other hand, fiction-making really is another kind of language game, then it is a strange sort of parasite that can't formally (in this case, i.e., textually or linguistically) be distinguished from its host. If there is no way formally to distinguish between host and parasite, it would seem to be an open question as to which indeed was the host and which the parasite. This is very much like the point on which Derrida finds Austin and Searle vulnerable. How, Derrida questions in effect, can we assert the logical priority of assertions seriously made over assertions made to deceive or as jokes? The fact that we can say something deceitfully or jokingly no more *derives* from the fact that we can assert something as true than the fact that we can assert things as true *derives* from the fact that we can assert things deceitfully or jokingly. Facts are as much parasites upon fictions as the other way around.[9]

Moreover, it hardly seems true that we need either in practice or in theory to resort to an author's intentions in order to identify a work as a work of fiction.[10] The phrase "once upon a time" would seem to be precisely a textual property conventionally taken to introduce a tale as fictional to small children just as the conventions of the omniscient narrator signal more grown-up readers that a work is fiction. Or perhaps I have not understood what Searle means by a "textual property."

Because pretending necessarily involves an intention to pretend, Searle concludes that only in that intention to pretend, which exists in the author's head and not in his texts, can we identify a work's fictionality. It is true that the phrase "once upon a time" need *not* introduce a fairy tale; it might introduce stories about parents and children when they were very much younger, for example. In this sense there is no formal or logical property in the phrase that points unequivocally toward truth or fiction. (Although in these cases the phrase certainly leans upon the tradition of fairy tales and makes fictionality at least a question.) But it is also true that someone who held the deluded belief that Mr. Pickwick was a real person or that there are people on Mars could write books about Mr. Pickwick and Martians that the author in no way intended to be fictional but that the rest of the world would read as such. Would we be wrong to read them as fictions? From this point of view it would seem that the reader's intentions are perhaps more determining than the author's. Suppose a reader who disbelieved in the real existence of Napoleon read and enjoyed a biography of Napoleon as a work of fiction. Would that be wrong? In the usual sense it would, but then this is just the sort of reading that literary people regularly do nowadays. The "wrong" reading might well have things to teach those committed to the existence of Napoleon, whereas it is harder to imagine the "wrong" reading of a nonfictionally intended book about Mr. Pickwick teaching anyone much at all.

Of course the usual sense of fiction has as its opposite not the "serious" (which is Searle's opposite and means intended to be taken as a view to which the author is committed), but the "factual." We know that there are good reasons to avoid the fact/fiction distinction, but a serious/nonserious distinction such as the one Searle offers is equally problematic—again, as Derrida has notably shown in writing about both Austin and Searle. Searle himself immediately feels the need to qualify his choice of terms by noting:

> To avoid one obvious sort of misunderstanding, this jargon is not meant to imply that writing a fictional novel or poem is not a serious activity, but rather that, for example, if the author of a novel tells us that it is raining outside he isn't seriously committed to the view that it is at the time of writing actually raining outside. It is in this sense that fiction is nonserious.[11]

If Searle wants to avoid the invidious distinction, why, especially in hunting around for a bit of jargon, hit upon so loaded a term as *nonserious*? (Or *parasitic* for that matter?)

Searle similarly seems to take with one hand what he has given with the other in his discussion of pretending. He has been discussing the randomly chosen first sentence of a novel (which in his example is Iris Murdoch's *The Red and the Green*). The novelist, he writes,

> is pretending, one could say, to make as assertion, or acting as if she were making an assertion, or going through the motions of making

an assertion, or imitating the making of an assertion. I place no great store by any of these verb phrases, but let us go to work on "pretend," as it is as good as any. When I say that Miss Murdoch is pretending to make an assertion, it is crucial to distinguish two quite different uses of "pretend." In one sense of "pretend," to pretend to do or be something that one is not doing is to engage in a form of deception, but in the second sense of "pretend," to pretend to do or be something is to engage in a performance which is *as if* one were doing or being the thing and is without any intent to deceive. If I pretend to be Nixon in order to fool the Secret Service into letting me into the White House, I am pretending in the first sense; if I pretend to be Nixon as part of a game of charades, it is pretending in the second sense. Now in the fictional use of words, it is pretending in the second sense which is in question. Miss Murdoch is engaging in a nondeceptive pseudo-performance which constitutes pretending to recount to us a series of events.[12]

If *pretend* is "as good as any," why immediately have to make an elaborate distinction between senses? The answer here I think is the same we would have to give in the case of the choice of "nonserious." Although he writes as though he has chosen his terms carelessly, no doubt Searle has in fact been thoughtful about them. There are good reasons why more appropriate terms are not at hand, for Searle is up against what I take to be a fundamental problem of fiction, and the problem responsible for what I have called the antinomy of literary probability: it is that in pretending (or entering a fictional world) something odd and complex happens to our beliefs about the things we pretend.

Explaining fictions by resorting to the idea of pretending does not solve anything if we deprive *pretend* of all its force by making it merely a matter of going through some motions or by rendering it "nonserious." Searle no doubt is *trying* to take fictions seriously, but one wonders what Murdoch would make of his description of her as "engaging in a nondeceptive pseudoperformance." Of course many dictionaries sanction Searle's separation of serious (or intended to deceive) and nonserious (intended not to deceive) senses of *pretend*. But as with the multiple senses of *probability*, are we not justified in looking for connections between those senses and in asking how or why their various senses have evolved? Moreover, even if we grant the justice of referring to different senses, it isn't evident how this explains anything. In the case of *pretend*, we find (in the *Oxford English Dictionary*) nothing very helpful in fact. There are a host of senses that are in Searle's terms nondeceptive and one that is not.[13] Out of the meaning "to put oneself forward in some character" evolves the meaning "to feign in play, to make believe." This latter sense interestingly appears only quite late, in 1865 (in *Alice in Wonderland*, appropriately enough). All that distinguishes this from other senses is the phrase "in play" and the phrase "make believe," which equal Searle's "nondeceptive." Searle's definition of fiction is effectively question begging (as is the dictionary's definition of *pretending*) in that it depends upon our already understanding the difference between an assertion intended to be taken as true and those intended as part of a game of make-believe. The history of the phrase *make believe* is not quite parallel to that of the senses of *pretend*, but it is equally unilluminating. A translation of the French *faire croire*, its first sense is serious and potentially deceptive, meaning "to cause people to believe" or "to stimulate a belief *that*." Sometime around the end of the eighteenth century this sense in general gives way to the modern one pertaining especially to "children in play," meaning "to subject oneself voluntarily to the illusion *that*." There is therefore an important shift away from the idea of making another believe something towards making oneself believe something. (The *OED*'s definition of *make believe* has the advantage of not being circular, but if we look at it closely it doesn't serve either. Someone who voluntarily subjected himself to an illusion would look just like Buonamici's madman, but this of course is not what people involved in the make-believe of fictions look like at all.)

There is something hollow about Searle's description of the novelist's fiction-making as "acting as if she were making an assertion, or going through the motions of making an assertion." It may be that when my children ask me to pretend to be the big bad wolf for the twelfth time at the end of a hard day I merely go through the motions of asserting that I'm the big bad wolf or act as if I were making that assertion. And in that case my children usually let me know it, for then there is something mechanical and false about my pretending. Searle has in fact been challenged on just this point by Kendall Walton, a philosopher who has written in the past ten years an important series of essays about fictions that ought to be better known among literary theorists than they seem to be.[14] Walton's argument will prove more useful to us than Derrida's because it takes the problems of pretending and fictional belief as central. He points out that while a novelist may be pretending to assert something, this state of mind has nothing to do with what makes the novelist's production fictional. He even questions whether fictions depend upon illocutionary acts or human acts at all:

> Consider a naturally occurring inscription of an assertive sentence, cracks in a rock, for example, which by pure coincidence spell out, "It is raining in Singapore," and suppose that we know for sure (somehow) that the cracks were formed naturally, that nobody inscribed (or used) them to assert anything. This inscription . . . would not convince us that it is raining in Singapore, or that there is reason to believe that it is, or that someone thinks that it is, or wants us to think so. . . .
>
> Contrast a naturally occurring "story," cracks in a rock, let us say, which spell out the words "once upon a time . . . [Walton's ellipses]," and so on. The realization that the inscription was not made or used by a person to tell a story need not prevent us from reading and enjoying the story in much the way we would if it were told by someone.[15]

Extreme (and fanciful) as this example is, it does for Walton show that there is a fundamental difference between the real-world discourse of illocutionary acts and fictional discourse. If Searle cannot quite decide if fiction really is a language game and a separate one at that, Walton is in no doubt. For him fictions are unambiguously and fundamentally different from the assertions made in the real world. Hence they cannot be said to be "parasitic" upon ordinary discourse, although he does grant that *literary* fictions, because they necessarily involve the use of language, may in a sense be said to be parasitic upon ordinary discourse because "perhaps nothing counts as language unless it is sometimes used for 'serious' discourse." A modernist or postmodernist might quarrel with that final bit of reasoning, but in any case this description would hold for fictional literary discourse, "merely because it is literature, not because it is fiction."[16] The parasitic relationship says nothing about the fictionality of fiction as such. (And fictions need not be linguistic at all, of course. One of the great merits of Walton's writings on fictions is that they encompass the plastic and performing arts as well as the literary.)

What becomes then of Searle's claim that novelists pretend to make assertions? In Walton's account, pretending remains a central character, but it properly belongs not (necessarily) to the fiction-maker but, as we have seen, to the fiction itself. So Walton would say that the maker of fictions doesn't pretend to make assertions at all; he really does make assertions (there is nothing "pretend" about the action of composing a novel, say), but ones that are themselves pretend. To begin a novel with the words "It was a dark and stormy night" is not to pretend to assert that it was a dark and stormy night. It is to assert really the fiction that it was a dark and stormy night, or, in Walton's preferred form, to say it is fictionally or make-believedly true that it was a dark and stormy night or most simply that it was fictionally a dark and stormy night.[17]

The difference between where Searle and Walton put the pretending in fiction-making may not seem earth-shattering to the nonlogician, but it does have important consequences. As we have already seen, to take Walton's view is to deny that fictions as such are parasitic upon ordinary discourse, to make fiction-making as such not a language game at all (so that to invoke speech-act theory does not allow us to say anything about fiction as such), and to allow therefore a kind of autonomy to fictional worlds that may go a long way towards restoring to them a degree of seriousness that Searle, for example, can't quite grant them in spite of his avowed intentions. To attribute the pretense to the fiction itself (and not to its maker), however, also significantly separates artist from audience in ways likely to make many readers, theorists, and historians uncomfortable. For in Walton's definition, "a work of fiction is a prop in a game of make-believe of certain sort, a game played by appreciators."[18] The fiction-maker *may* be in various ways earnestly committed to his fictions and *may* feel himself to be in close relationship with his audience, but then again he *need* not be. As makers of fictions, there is no essential difference between such types as the novelist, the designer of dolls (or toys of any kind), and the pornographer. The maker of novels, that is, like the toy-maker and the pornographer, need not play the game he creates at all.

And there is a further consequence of Walton's view, implicit in the example of the naturally occurring fiction, that really is startling—and likely to be controversial. If the fictionality of a thing doesn't necessarily depend upon a human maker, then *style,* which does depend upon a human maker, in Walton's account

> is not *intrinsic* or *essential* to fictional representation. We can consider the fictional world and the apparent action of creating the work separately. In understanding a work of fiction we do not *need* to think of it as a vehicle of someone's action, as something with a style. In this sense *style* can be separated from *content.* "Serious" discourse allows no such separation. Nonfictional utterances are *essentially* vehicles of illocutionary actions and essentially have styles. They cannot be understood except as having styles.[19]

But for our purposes the significance of Walton's view is that it keeps us focused on the fact of pretending or make-believe. I think that his view enormously clarifies many of the confusions in a view like Searle's, but the question we must now put to it is: Does it help us understand what the nature of make-believe is?

Here Walton seems to me less successful, though it is instructive to look closely at his efforts along these lines. His most relevant essays are a pair of articles called "Fearing Fictions" and "How Remote are Fictional Worlds from the Real World?" The first of these asks what *psychological* connections there are between real and fictional worlds by imagining a person (called Charles) who is watching a scene in a horror movie in which a blob of green slime is oozing its way toward the camera and throwing Charles into an apparent fright. The second poses what seems at first to be an entirely silly question about what *physical* connections there can be between real and fictional worlds. What is for me most valuable about these essays is that they examine the question of one's belief in fictions quite seriously and try to say something about fictions based upon that examination. By imagining Charles's psychological reaction to the green slime and noting that it really does look like genuine fear, Walton is in effect asking how far the audience of art may be like Buonamici's madman and how much that audience really may be said to believe in the representations presented to it.

Walton is especially clear-sighted in his recognition on the one hand that Charles is *not* Buonamici's madman and in his criticisms on the other hand of the loose way we usually have of talking about literary belief. He knows that in some sense Charles is not deceived at all by the illusion in front of him, and yet he recognizes that Charles's responses are not the sort one has to things one doesn't believe in either.

> Defenders of the claim that Charles is afraid may argue that Charles *does* believe that the green slime is real and is a real threat to him. There are, to be sure, strong reasons for allowing that Charles realizes that the slime is only fictional and poses no danger. If he didn't we should expect him to flee the theater, call the police, warn his family. But perhaps it is *also* true that Charles believes, in some way or "on some level," that the slime is real and really threatens him. It has been said that in cases like this one "suspends one's disbelief" or that "part" of a person believes something which another part of him disbelieves, or that one finds oneself (almost?) believing something one nevertheless knows to be false. . . .
>
> One possibility is that Charles half believes that there is a real danger, and that he is, literally, at least half afraid. To half believe something is to be not quite sure that it is true, but also not quite sure that it is not true. But Charles has *no* doubts about whether he is in the presence of an actual slime. If he half believed, and were

half afraid, we would expect him to have *some* inclination to act on his fear in the normal ways. Even a hesitant belief, a mere suspicion, that the slime is real would induce any normal person seriously to consider calling the police and warning his family. Charles gives no thought whatsoever to such courses of action. He is not *uncertain* whether the slime is real; he is perfectly sure that it is not.[20]

And yet there are those distinct and even measurable signs of fear: breathlessness, a pounding heart, and Charles's grasping his chair until his knuckles are white. Walton supposes one might, faced with this contradiction, claim that there is a distinction to be made between Charles's "intellectual" and "gut" beliefs, like those of the phobic who knows the statistics about the safety of flying but still cannot bring himself to get on a plane. But as Walton points out, the phobic's beliefs about the danger of flying do actually lead to actions on his part, the actions of avoiding travel by plane. Charles, on the contrary, "does not have even an inclination to leave the theater or call the police." The phobic's actions are deliberate and therefore can be attributed to beliefs, whereas Charles's actions are automatic and therefore lie outside the realm of reason and belief.[21] Another explanation might be that Charles's belief, instead of being partial, is really momentary: "These moments are too short for Charles to think about doing anything; so (one might claim) it isn't surprising that his belief and fear are not accompanied by the normal inclinations to act." Walton finds this last move "unconvincing," because Charles's responses are in fact not momentary, but may last for quite long stretches—certainly for periods long enough in which to contemplate and execute actions.[22] He might have added that the kinds of action appropriate to confronting green slime in fact hardly require a moment's thought in any case.

Walton's criticisms of these kinds of accounts lead him to a conclusion that we might already have sensed from his definition of fictions as props in games of make-believe. It is that Charles's fear is itself make-believe, a part of the game of fiction:

Charles believes (he knows) that make-believedly the green slime is bearing down on him and he is in danger of being destroyed by it. His quasi-fear results from this belief. What makes it make-believe that he is afraid rather than angry or excited or upset is the fact that his quasi-fear is caused by the belief that make-believedly he is in danger. And his belief that make-believedly it is the slime that endangers him is what makes it make-believe that the slime is the object of his fear. In short, my suggestion is this: the fact that Charles is quasi-afraid as a result of realizing that make-believedly the slime threatens him generates the truth that make-believedly he is afraid of the slime.[23]

Thus we return to Walton's definition of fictions as props used in games of make-believe. Charles's fear itself is a fiction, itself becomes a prop that keeps the game going. In considering the audience for fictions, we can now say that just as the fiction-maker really makes assertions, but make-believe ones, so too the audience really have reactions, but make-believe ones. In this connection Walton quotes Borges: "[The actor] on a stage plays at being another person before a gathering of people who play at taking him for that other person."[24] Rather than say Charles is really afraid or even really has a psychological attitude toward the fictions represented in the film, Walton would have us say rather that Charles is make-believedly afraid. (This of course does not mean he cannot also pretend to be really afraid, as for example when he shouts, "Yikes, here it comes!")[25]

Again, it may not be immediately obvious why such a formulation is all that much better than others—why it is so terrible after all to say that Charles's fear is real or that he has real psychological attitudes towards the slime or characters in the movie. Walton confronts the dangers he sees in such latter expressions more directly in "How Remote are Fictional Worlds from the Real World?" which he begins with several examples of playful and highly self-conscious self-reference in fiction, ranging from Mel Brooks and Woody Allen to Julio Cortazar and Samuel Beckett. In all of these, play is made out of the apparent possibility of real (that is, physical) interaction between real and fictional worlds. In the shortest and simplest example, a character in *Blazing Saddles* orders a cab driver, "Drive me off this picture."[26] Although it seems an absurd question for anyone to ask, Walton wants to know if there is anything to the possibility of such interactions. And in the process of answering that question he poses some very interesting puzzles of his own devising. He asks us to consider for example "the classic story of Henry, a backwoods villager watching a theatrical performance, who leaps to the stage to save the heroine from the clutches of the villain and a horrible death."[27] This of course is our old acquaintance Buonamici's madman or imbecile, but our interest here is not with his mental state (as it was in the case of Charles and the green slime); it is rather upon the question of *what happens to the fiction* when Henry really does leap to the stage and save the heroine. Does that real action then generate any fictional truths, such as that Henry has saved the heroine, and does that mean he has actually entered the fictonal world of the heroine? If one protests that Henry has not really done anything to the play itself, but only interfered with a particular performance of it, then of course Henry has other means of apparently saving the heroine available to him. "The thing to do is to catch the author in the act of writing the play and force him, at gunpoint if necessary, to spare the heroine."[28]

But Walton pushes this argument to the point at which the "isolation of fictional worlds from the real world seems to have vanished" only to refute it.[29] What makes the argument seem plausible is first of all a confusion about the nature of fictions, a confusion that the definition we have examined above clears up. Physical (or psychological) interaction between real and fictional worlds seems possible only if we take fictional statements (like, "Tom Sawyer attended his own funeral," or, "Robinson Crusoe was shipwrecked") "at face value" and "treat them as the straightforward subject/predicate statements they appear to be." To take this view is to take Robinson Crusoe, for example, as an entity that has real existence and can possess such ordinary properties as being shipwrecked; how otherwise could he be referred to?[30] Against this position, which is usual among those who write about fictions, Walton suggests that to say, "Robinson Crusoe survived a shipwreck," "is not to attribute to Crusoe the property of having survived a shipwreck, to claim that he, literally, possesses that property; it is not to refer to Crusoe at all nor to attribute any property to him."[31] Instead, Walton proposes that such statements are really elliptical, a kind of shorthand for, "In the novel, *Robinson Crusoe,* Crusoe survived a shipwreck," or, better, and familiar already from our discussion above, elliptical for, "It is fictional that Crusoe survived." Such a statement

> Should be regarded as analogous to statements such as the following:
>
> > It is believed that Jones survived.
> > It is claimed that Jones survived.
> > It is wished that Jones survived.
> > It is denied that Jones survived.
>
> These are used not to assert that the proposition that Jones survived is true, but to attribute other properties to it, to assert that this proposition is believed, or that someone claims, or wishes, or denies, it to be true.[32]

The practical advantage of this view is for Walton that it clears up once and for all the logical confusion between real and fictional worlds that ensues when we assume that statements about fictional entities refer to actually existent entities, an assumption that makes possible such puzzles as the self-conscious and self-referring crack "Drive me off this picture" or Walton's questions about whether Henry's leaping to the stage to save the heroine actually constitutes his entering her fictional world. Given Walton's view, the puzzles evaporate. Thus he can say about the question of Henry's "saving" the heroine that it is not "fictional" that Henry saves the heroine because

> it is not fictional that he exists, and it cannot be fictional that one does any saving unless fictionally one exists. There is no understanding (in traditional theater) whereby Henry's action counts as his fictionally saving the heroine. His behavior is understood not as part of the theatrical event, but as an intrusion on it.

What *is* true is that Henry makes it fictional that the heroine survives. He arranges things in such a way that this fictional truth is generated. But doing this is not *saving* the heroine, neither literally nor fictionally. Henry brings it about that fictionally the heroine survives, but he does not save her, and it is not fictional that he saves her.[33]

There can no longer be any question of Henry's entering a fictional world: the real world and fictional worlds are therefore in this sense infinitely remote, and the "notion of an unbridgeable gulf separating fictional worlds from the real world is thus neatly vindicated."[34]

To the appreciator of fictions (i.e., to me), there is something disappointing in this last conclusion, as there is something disappointing too in the conclusion that Charles isn't really afraid, but only make-believedly so when he is confronted by the green slime. Walton begins by apparently taking fictions very seriously—as did Searle—yet he ends—as did Searle—by undermining the idea that we have anything we could call real belief in them. Indeed, though he generally writes as though he takes fictions much *more* seriously than Searle—defending them for example against the idea that they are merely parasitic upon our discourse about real things—he goes much further than Searle in fact in distancing fictions from the real world. By taking the pretending away from the fiction-maker and ascribing it to the things he makes (by saying that the fiction-maker really asserts a pretend thing instead of saying the fiction-maker pretends to assert a real thing), Walton disrupts the connection we usually assume between the fiction-maker and his audience. As we have seen, this move makes it possible for there to be fictions without any maker at all and therefore of course denies that there is any necessary connection between the imaginative world of the fiction-maker and his audience. But it isn't just this dehumanizing of the activity of fiction-making, the denial that it need be an "act" at all, that is likely to disappoint. Walton denies fictions any kind of truth like the truth that we know about the real world,[35] denies that they occupy "worlds" analogous to the real "world," denies indeed that they contain things that exist at all, denies that we can be said to have psychological attitudes toward them at all. Thus he can write of a playgoer who finds himself wanting to see the heroine saved, "It is merely make-believe that the spectator sympathizes with the heroine and wants her to escape."[36] What could be more dismissive than this?

Walton in fact does not mean to be dismissive of fictions, but he is led to write as he does of them because his concern is ultimately with their logical status, and in his logical account of fictions necessarily they do come out looking absolutely untrue, unreal, and otherworldly—or rather non-worldly. But that ought really to surprise no one. What is surprising indeed from most perspectives is that anyone should ever have thought otherwise, that there should even be logicians considering other possibilities (such as trying to make fictional entities existent things we can really refer to). Walton does not want to be dismissive of fictions, because while his logical interests may be primary, they are not his only interests and cannot in fact entirely be separated from what we should perhaps call his psychological ones. While he is interested in making various puzzles evaporate, he is at the same time attentive to the fact that there is something about these puzzles that resists solution, or rather that there is something in *us* that resists seeing them solved.

Walton, like Searle, makes pretending (or make-believe) the central feature of his account. He does better than Searle at not taking for granted an understanding of what pretending is, but his account falls very short of being a thorough examination of what make-believe is or how it operates. And Walton seems to understand both this and that a full understanding of fictions would require such an examination. He notes a curious fact about the way we talk about fictional entities that undermines his own analogy between the statement "It is fictional that . . ." and statements that begin with intentional operators like, "It is believed that . . . ," or, "It is denied that . . . ," and so on. The fact is that we commonly leave out the "it is fictional that," whereas it would be extremely rare for us to leave out an "it is believed that":

Even when it is clearly understood that one is speaking about Jone's wishes it would be very unnatural to say merely, "A golden mountain will appear on the horizon," meaning that Jones wishes a golden mountain would appear on the horizon. Occasionally "It is believed that" or "He says that" is omitted, but only in fairly special circumstances. And I know of no ordinary situations in which one might say "Smith robbed the bank" as an abbreviation for "It is denied (or, "It is denied by Jones") that Smith robbed the bank."[37]

And there is another phenomenon as well that Walton thinks provides good evidence for the *dis*analogy between fictional and other kinds of operators. It is that in German a speaker ordinarily uses the indicative in speaking about matters of fact and the subjunctive in speaking about things contrary to fact. But this practice is suspended when one speaks about fictional events, for in German one customarily speaks about these in the indicative.[38] Why should this be? Walton's answer to the puzzles posed by these phenomena has nothing to do with logic:

> The explanation lies in our habit of playing along with fictions, or make-believedly asserting, pretending to assert, what we know to be only make-believedly the case. We mustn't be too quick to assume that an utterance of '*p*' is merely an ellipsis for 'Make-believedly *p*' (or 'In the novel *p*'). This assumption is wrong if the speaker make-believedly is asserting that *p*, rather than (or in addition to) asserting that make-believedly *p*. Charles's frantic, "Yikes, here it comes!" is an obvious case in point. A case only slightly less obvious is that of a person reading *The Adventures of Tom Sawyer* who remarks, gravely and with an expression of deep concern, that Tom and Becky are lost in a cave.
>   I do not suggest that the omission of 'in the novel' is *never* a mere ellipsis. "Tom and Becky were lost in a cave" uttered by a critic analyzing the novel could easily have been expanded to "In the novel Tom and Becky were lost in a cave" without altering the character of the remark. . . . But our habit of dropping fictional operators persists even in sober criticism, and testifies to the ease with which we can be induced to play along, deliberately, with a work of fiction.[39]

Walton knows that his appeal to "our habit of playing along with fictions" leaves a good deal still unexplained. "An explanation is needed," he says, "for our strangely persistent inclination to think of fictions as sharing reality with us."[40] What impedes the logical analysis of fictions therefore is in a sense not something intrinsic to the nature of fictions themselves, in other words, but some psychological fact about ourselves. We all really do know that the fictions are merely fictional, but we persist in treating them as real. We persist in our game of make-believe.

I am not about to offer an explanation for why people persist in playing games of make-believe, but I would like to try for a description of what happens in games of make-believe such that we do not begin by taking them seriously only to wind up dismissing them as make-believe things—which we of course always knew they were anyway. Walton himself is aware of just such a danger, although I think he succumbs to it necessarily by virtue of his interest in the *logic* of fictions. He begins, in his own terminology, as an appreciator, but he is compelled by the force of his own logic to end as a detractor.[41] Yet at the end of "How Remote are Fictional Worlds from the Real World?" he provides us, in an undeveloped insight, with an important tool for creating a less dismissive description of make-believe:

> When readers and spectators become fictional [that is, when readers and spectators enter fictional worlds by pretending to believe in them] they do not of course cease to be actual. If a reader or spectator is such that fictionally he exists, it is also literally the case that he exists. So our standpoint is a dual one. We, as it were, see Tom Sawyer *both* from inside his world and from outside of it. And we do so simultaneously. The reader is such that, fictionally, he knows that Tom attended his own funeral, and he is such that fictionally he worries about Tom and Becky in the cave. At the same time the reader knows that no such persons as Tom and Becky ever existed.[42]

It is, I believe, on this point about the duality of the fiction-player's perspective that an account of our belief in fictions ought really to be based. If indeed an appreciation of the duality of our standpoint is what will avoid the typical confusions experienced by writers about fiction, it is also an appreciation of that duality that will prevent us from writing about fictions as *mere* make-believe, for to write thus is to ignore one perspective of the dual standpoint—to pretend that we do not pretend. Let us therefore make that duality the very center of our description. In doing so, we shall have to cover some of the territory already explored by Searle and Walton again, but our goal is an important one. If we can't hope to say why people persist in make-believe, we may be able to contribute something to our understanding of just what make-believe entails.

To talk about one's belief in fictions (poetic or otherwise) as though it were a kind of intermediate belief is, as we have seen Walton point out, not quite right. Coleridge, for example, on occasion writes thus, and Coleridge is one of the few writers before the twentieth century to discuss the logic of fictional belief—as opposed, say, to the constituents of fictional belief—at any length. He writes in some well-known remarks about the aims of the drama (apropos *The Tempest*):

> Here I find two extremes in critical decision: the French, which evidently presupposes that a perfect delusion is to be aimed at—an opinion which now needs no fresh confutation; the opposite, supported by Dr. Johnson, supposes the auditors throughout as in the full and positive reflective knowledge of the contrary. In evincing the impossibility of delusion, he makes no sufficient allowance for an intermediate state, which we distinguish by the term illusion.
>
> In what this consists I cannot better explain than by referring you to the highest degree of it; namely, dreaming. It is laxly said that during sleep we take our dreams for realities, but this is irreconcilable with the nature of sleep, which consists in a suspension of the voluntary and, therefore, of the comparative power. The fact is that we pass no judgement either way: we simply do not judge them to be unreal, in consequence of which the images act on our minds, as far as they act at all, by their own force as images. Our state while we are dreaming differs from that in which we are

in the perusal of a deeply interesting novel in the degree rather than
in the kind.[43]

These remarks usefully explain Coleridge's more famous formula
about "that willing suspension of disbelief for the moment, which
constitutes poetic faith."[44] They seem to me precisely right in rejecting
the extreme positions of both the French neoclassicals and Dr. Johnson
and correct too in their observation about the psychology of dreams
that in dreaming we don't accept the reality of the dream so much as
simply fail to make any judgment.[45] But is also seems quite wrong to
posit a belief that we have in fictions "intermediate" between absolute
credulity on the one hand and absolute rejection on the other. For one
thing, such an expression supposes a spectrum of belief which has
certain knowledge at one end, ignorance at the other, and degrees of
more or less probable knowledge all throughout the middle. No one,
surely, imagines a spectrum of *actual* readers with the French neoclassicals, credulous imbeciles, and madmen at one end, the complete
skeptics (including Dr. Johnson) refusing their assent to any degree of
truth to fictions at the other, and the contented bulk of the intermedi-
ately believing, quasidreaming, play-going-poetry-and-novel-reading
public in the middle. One problem with such a spectrum is that the
whole spectrum in effect accepts the *terms* of the madman's or imbecile's
belief: it can only be a spectrum describing belief in the literal factuality
of the fiction, and indeed such a spectrum really has no middle. It is
not, that is, a spectrum at all, but simply the familiar opposition between on the one hand the mad and imbecile who (and only who, of
course) are taken in by the claim of fictions to tell the literal truth and
on the other hand everybody else, the people who cannot see anything
to believe in stories as well as those who can. A spectrum has a middle;
an opposition cannot. The quarrels among readers neither mad nor
imbecile clearly have nothing to do with the literal fidelity of fictions to
the world of fact, even if that has sometimes seemed to be the case,
precisely because of our habit of pretending that fictional worlds are
real ones. Another problem with the spectrum is evident in Coleridge's
analogy with dreaming: the very fact that he turns to a qualitatively

different psychological state suggests that he is not really discussing a single spectrum at all. Logically, the middle of a spectrum with believers at one end and disbelievers at the other has at its center probabilists of one kind or another. But by his own account dreamers make no epistemological judgments at all.

How then else can we characterize the nature of our belief in fictions? If it does not seem right to lump the enthusiastic novel reader with the skeptic down at belief degree zero, and if the fiction-reader's belief is at the same time not intermediate or partial, surely it is not anything we would want to call belief *entire* either, is it? Or if we reject the idea of such a spectrum altogether are we not then in a situation vis-à-vis belief precisely analogous to that we found ourselves in vis-à-vis probability and which we wanted to avoid: that of having to make a radical distinction between literary and all other kinds of belief—a distinction that takes with one hand what it gives with the other by saying *this* kind of belief really isn't belief anyway? And if literary belief really *is* belief, then perhaps we really do want to say that it can be belief entire. Is then the answer to the question whether literary belief is entire belief both yes and no?

It helps to step back and recall what we actually see in a person intently reading—or watching a play or a movie, for that matter, as Walton has done with his imaginary Charles. We have all observed someone apparently completely absorbed in the world of a book who then proceeds to demonstrate a simultaneous and perfect awareness of what we call the real world by unerringly reaching out and, say, picking up a glass. Or we have seen moviegoers like Charles who in the very act of exclaiming, "Yikes, here it comes!" dip into the popcorn box. No doubt we have also seen instances in which the spell of reading is interrupted by such actions as well as instances in which the reader with perfect unconsciousness misses the popcorn box altogether. But the point—and it is I believe definitive of the sort of play involved in entertaining fictions—is that even the most deeply absorbed reader can and does for the most part *divide* attention between the two worlds and gets along reasonably well in each at the same time.

It is again in this *division*—the dual standpoint of the reader or playgoer—that we need to look for our understanding of literary belief and the answer to the question of whether such belief really is fundamentally belief after all and therefore whether it is belief entire.

Let us return to a point Walton makes about his imaginary Charles. We have seen that on the way to arguing that we can have no real psychological attitudes toward fictions, Walton argues that Charles has *no* belief in the slime: neither a half-belief nor even so much as a shred of doubt. He argues thus on the reasonable grounds that Charles takes no action we might expect from someone who was in any real doubt at all.[46] The incommensurability of or contradiction between Charles's certainty that the slime is not real and what Walton calls his "quasi-fear" (real somatic signs of excitement like a quickened pulse and white knuckles) become powerful agents in the argument because that contradiction points to the unreality both of the belief and of the fear. For the fear is apparently so great that it would if real have to accompany real doubt about the slime's existence. That Charles does not call the police in spite of his exhibiting all the symptoms of real fear is for Walton an important sign that the fear is not after all real. But it is just this question we need to examine more closely. For if it turns out that Charles's fear is real in some sense, then that would suggest that his belief too is in some sense real, because to have a real fear of something would imply a real belief in it.

Walton has chosen his imaginary subject Charles well. He is obviously a boy old enough really to know that green slime is an imaginary commodity, but young enough to play the game of pretend in ways that make it easy for us to see him playing it—or hearing him, as when he says, "Yikes, here it comes!" Charles does not seem to be psychologically at all vulnerable, and evidently the slime is not going to engender nightmares. That is convenient for Walton just because his point is that we do not in fact have real psychological attitudes toward fictional entities any more than we have real physical interactions with them. Nevertheless, Walton seems at points to suspect a weakness in his case. He refers to Charles's "quasi-fear" and speculates in a footnote: "One can't help wondering why Charles's realization that make-believedly he is in danger produces quasi-fear in him, why it brings about a state similar to real fear, even though he knows he is not really in danger."[47] But he is happiest dismissing the reality of the fear altogether, even on an occasion when he imagines someone considerably younger than Charles doing the pretending:

> Compare Charles with a child playing an ordinary game of make-believe with his father. The father, pretending to be a ferocious monster, cunningly stalks the child and, at a critical moment, lunges viciously at him. The child flees, screaming, to the next room. The scream is more or less involuntary, and so is the flight. But the child has a delighted grin on his face even while he runs, and he unhesitatingly comes back for more. He is perfectly aware that his father is only "playing," that the whole thing is "just a game," and that only make-believedly is there a vicious monster after him. He is not really afraid.[48]

To which I have to reply: well, sometimes. But sometimes too the fear looks entirely real. Surely if we were to offer a full theory of make-believe it would include an account of such games as one of the child's ways of coping with real fears (even if they include as their objects merely imaginary possibilities), and surely there are plenty of times in such games when fear gets the upper hand, the child's delighted grin disappears, and the child begs tearfully to stop. At such moments the child may still clearly "know" the game is just a game and yet be "really afraid." But it is not just in someone younger than Charles that the fear looks real. As grown-ups reading fictions we are apt to resent the suggestion that our feelings for Emma Woodhouse, say, are simply make-believe, if that is understood to mean that our feelings for Emma therefore are psychologically unreal. It is just this point that seems to have inspired Harold Skulsky's rebuttal of Walton, and while I cannot say I agree with the logic of Skulsky's analysis, it does seem to me that this is Walton's most vulnerable point.[49]

A weakness of Skulsky's argument is that it fails to understand the dual standpoint of the make-believer in Walton's account.[50] But perhaps so too does Walton in this instance. Indeed, I suspect that Walton's questioning the reality of Charles's fear is itself the product of his failure to take into account the dual standpoint of the moviegoer. From the standpoint of Charles in the fictional world, his fear may—indeed, must—be perfectly real and result in all the usual consequences of fear. If it is not real from this standpoint, then where is the make-believe? But from the standpoint of Charles outside the fictional world, the fear of course does not lead to the consequences in action that we would expect from Charles if he took the slime to be real slime. Walton would perhaps counter that the quasifear Charles feels could be described as real fear of the depiction, not real fear of the thing that was depicted. There is truth in this, but insofar as this is simply saying the thing depicted was fictional and therefore could not be the object of fear (in Walton's account, and just as it could not actually be referred to), it is true only circularly. Walton again seems aware of possible objections on this point, and he imagines an older Charles with a bad heart who is afraid that a scary movie will bring on a heart attack; he writes of this older moviegoer that "perhaps he knows that any excitement could trigger a heart attack and fears that the movie will cause excitement, e.g., by depicting the green slime as being especially aggressive or threatening. This is real fear. But it is fear of the depiction of the slime, not fear of the slime that is depicted."[51] But this is not satisfying. Walton would surely to be consistent have to argue that the "excitement" felt by the older Charles was, insofar as it was a psychological as well as a somatic state, just like the younger Charles's "quasifear," not "real" excitement at all, but only make-believe excitement. But how can merely make-believe excitement bring on a real heart attack? Is this older Charles not then having a real psychological attitude toward a make-believe entity? Walton's example again is cleverly chosen, for the word *excitement* seems to denote a merely somatic state, even though if we think about it, it must have a psychological component; it is excitement accompanying or identified with *thoughts* about fictional objects. It would seem then that we have to reject his conclusion that real psychological attitudes toward fictional entities are impossible.[52]

It is easy to sympathize with Walton's worry here, for if we have real psychological attitudes toward fictions and real beliefs about them, then that would seem to open up once again the absurd possibility of bridging the gap between the two worlds and actually leaving one and entering the other. But there are other ways to close off that possibility than to deny the reality of our psychological attitudes or beliefs. Walton is no doubt right to reject such formulations as Coleridge's about "intermediate" belief, but Coleridge is right too, as Walton for the most part knows, to reject both the extreme theories that people involved with fictions are on the one hand either entirely taken in or on the other entirely untouched by the illusion. The error comes in supposing that we ever live entirely in one world or the other.

It seems a better and simpler description to take our cue from the dual standpoint as Walton has discovered it and say simply that *in entertaining fictions (or making believe) we divide our beliefs between real and fictional worlds.* It is only as a manner of speaking that there is a question of a gap between worlds: the "real" gap is within ourselves. We can retain Walton's view that statements like, "Mr Pickwick was bald," are elliptical for, "It is fictional that Mr. Pickwick was bald," or, "Mr. Pickwick was make-believedly bald," and like Walton we can resist saying that this is *all* they could be. For as he points out, when we actually pretend, these statements are not elliptical at all. But our understanding of such fictional operators would not lead us to such conclusions as Walton's that the gap between fictional and real worlds is absolute and unbridgeable, or that fictional entities do not exist, or that we cannot have real psychological attitudes towards fictional entities, for these conclusions are true only insofar as we refuse to play the game of make-believe and therefore effectively ignore the make-believer's dual perspective. From the dual standpoint of the make-believer it is simultaneously true that I believe Mr. Pickwick is bald and that I believe there never was a Mr. Pickwick, so he could not possibly have been bald; that I can see Mr. Pickwick now (that we are in the same world), and that there is no possibility of my ever seeing Mr. Pickwick (because our worlds are unbridgeable). These apparently contradictory beliefs are contradictory only from the standpoint of one who refuses to pretend. It may be objected that sober philosophy and criticism ought precisely to adopt the standpoint of refusing to pretend, but I cannot think of any good reasons why this actually should be. Walton's sober philosophy would not be possible if he never allowed himself to pretend, and I cannot see that the sober critic's responsibility is not to pretend. Surely it is only to be as clear as possible about when he pretends and about what is pretended. Indeed, it is not at all obvious that there are psychological states in which pretending is not at some level or to some degree going on, although that raises a new question. Surely it puts one in as false a position to pretend that one does not pretend as it does simply to pretend.

What should by now be clear from our discussion of belief is that an essential part of reading stories or of entertaining any kind of make-believe is "having it both ways." It is insisting on our belief in the fictional world *even as* we insist also on our belief in the world in which the reading or make-believe takes place. We recognize a fundamental distinction between the qualities of these beliefs, and yet this distinction ought not to become what it seems inevitably always to become, a distinction that invalidates one kind of belief as lesser, as not really "belief" after all.

Of course there is a problem with "having it both ways." We recognize that from some perspectives one cannot have it both ways, that there is something fundamentally impossible about having it both ways. Every student in an introductory course in logic knows that having it both ways violates the law of the excluded middle, which says that something cannot at once be *p* and *not-p*. But this does not invalidate our description of reading; it simply says, again, as Plato knew perfectly well, that there is a problem about entertaining fictions.[53] And the problem, we can now say, is that the answer to the question with which we began (Is our belief in fictions belief entire or no?) turns out to be—our conventional understanding of logic notwithstanding—both yes and no.

Yes, it is belief entire if we mean belief that is not something *less* than belief, that is, not a belief lessened by doubt. No, it is not belief entire if we mean belief that is monolithic, belief that is undivided and leaves room for no other perhaps contradictory beliefs. We could of course simply decide that "belief" is an equivocal word and split it up—thinking of an analogy with the problem of probability and following, say, the example of Carnap—into belief$_1$ (for belief about things in the "real" world) and belief$_2$ (for belief about fictions and fantasies). But this isn't very satisfactory because, like probability$_1$ and probability$_2$, the concepts in practice simply will not stay apart. There will be disagreements of course about what constitutes the real and fictional worlds in any case, but most importantly we cannot split the word up for all the reasons already suggested: because to split belief up into two concepts inevitably is to deny them unity and therefore to deny that they are both *really* belief; belief$_2$ inevitably would come to be taken (or in the minds of many even begin by being taken) as something *less* than belief$_1$, and it would require no very clever child to learn to see behind such apparently bland statements as, "I have belief$_1$ in the physical reality of the book and belief$_2$ in the three little pigs," the rhetoric of the killjoy and the determination to prevent us from "having it both ways." The distinction is one that cannot help but become invidious, and it is a distinction that effectively prevents us from pretending.

In order to pretend that something is real one must in some sense take it as real, behave—even if one's behavior is entirely internal and unobservable by an outsider—as though one believes it is real; otherwise there is no pretending going on. But at the same time in pretending we do not lose touch with the world in which our pretend is going on, we do not become deluded in fact. To pretend as we do in reading fiction is therefore necessarily to keep alive a tension between the real and fictional worlds, a tension that is absent in madmen and imbeciles, as well as in the advocates of belief$_1$ and belief$_2$; for the mad and imbecile lose the tension in seeing no distinction between real and fictional worlds, while the believers in subscripts would maintain a separation that is complete and absolute. (The Walton who concludes that the gap between real and fictional worlds is complete and unbridgeable feels no such tension; the Walton who reads and writes fictional sentences and otherwise engages in games of make-believe does.)

Division, having it both ways, tension: these are the strands that run through this description of reading fictions, and they have in common, of course, duality or doubleness. A major point of this argument is to insist upon that doubleness, to prevent us from letting ourselves forget it. It is to insist on a division we may speak about as either in ourselves or in our world, as opposed to a doubleness (equivocality) in the concept *belief.* But the argument recognizes too that it is up against the intractable fact that readers of course will in practice forget the doubleness and in some way conflate the two worlds—not as the mad and imbecile would do, but by having it both ways: as I shall do the next time I think seriously about David Copperfield, say. Readers will insist upon a fundamental unity between literary and other kinds of belief and will make serious play out of the doubleness of the reader's world. They *will* forget (or pretend to forget) that the big bad wolf and David Copperfield are not real even as they will not forget to turn the pages of the book before them: even as they forget (or pretend to forget) the fictionality of the fiction, that is, they will at the very same time *not* forget the claims of the real world. Not only is the reader's world double, as we have described it, but the reader himself is double.

Plenty of other writers have arrived at descriptions of readers as divided beings. Here for example is Roland Barthes at the beginning of *The Pleasure of the Text:*

> Imagine someone . . . who abolishes within himself all barriers, all classes, all exclusions, not by syncretism but by simple discard of that old specter: *logical contradiction*; who mixes every language, even those said to be incompatible; who silently accepts every change of illogicality, of incongruity; who remains passive in the face of Socratic irony (leading the interlocutor to the supreme disgrace: *self-contradiction*). . . . Such a man would be the mockery of our society: court, school, asylum, polite conversation would cast him out: who endures contradiction without shame? Now this anti-hero exists: he is the reader of the text at the moment he takes his pleasure. Thus the Biblical myth is reversed, the confusion

of tongues is no longer a punishment, the subject gains access to bliss by the cohabitation of languages *working side by side:* the text of pleasure is a sanctioned Babel.[54]

Clearly an important and worthwhile part of Barthes's aim is by a by-now familiar one: to defamiliarize our picture of the normal reader. But one implication of this extravagant rhetoric is that the reader actively *rebels* against principles of logic and order. The tension or division we have been discussing within the reader is however not produced by an act of rebellion; it does not follow out of any act committed *against* some other kind of reading but rather is a condition of the act of reading itself and, more fundamentally, a condition of the act of pretending itself. It is there already as the normal condition of a two-year-old listening to a bedtime story.

And yet we do not want too commonsensical a description of this division either. Jonathan Culler has written some of the best accounts of the divisions within readers as well as the most detailed and intelligent accounts of other writers who assume divided readers (writers like Wolfgang Iser, Stanley Fish, Norman Holland, and Peter Rabinowitz, for example).[55] Here is one of his typically lucid portrayals of the divided reader:

> To read is to play the role of a reader and to interpret is to posit an experience of reading. This is something that beginning literature students know quite well but have forgotten by the time they get to graduate school and begin teaching literature. When student papers refer to what "the reader feels here" or what "the reader then understands," teachers often take this as a spurious objectivity, a disguised form of "I feel" or "I understand," and urge their charges either to be honest or to omit such references. But students know better than their teachers here. They know it is not a matter of honesty. They have understood that to read and interpret literary works is precisely to imagine what "a reader" would feel and understand. To read is to operate with the hypothesis of a reader, and there is always a gap or division within reading.[56]

This is all perfectly consistent with—indeed, reminiscent of—Kendall Walton's account of the dual standpoint occupied by readers and how they become themselves fictional when they are immersed in fictional worlds. But both Walton's and Culler's way of writing also undermines the very distinction that is being portrayed. Here and elsewhere Culler stresses that the division in reading involves not just a split in readers but the creation of a new, fictional reader. "The fiction of a reader," he writes, "is absolutely central to the reading of fiction."[57] As in Walton's account, and as in the assertion that "to read is to operate with the hypothesis of a reader," there is an implication here that the division in reading is itself fictional or hypothetical. There are not *really* two readers, we might say, but rather a primary, real reader and a secondary, fictional reader who is produced by the fictional division that comes about when we pretend. I hope that by now it is clear that this description is true only from the standpoint we adopt when we pretend not to pretend, the standpoint that therefore fails to take seriously the division we have been working so hard to uphold. I want to maintain of course that we must take Culler's hypothetical reader as seriously (or as "nonfictionally") as we take his primary reader.

We are at a point at which the logical touches the psychological. The paradoxes of fictionality appear in logic because logic does not allow us to entertain contradictory opinions or view things from two quite different standpoints at the same time. Psychology does, at least to the extent that it admits phenomena involving splits in our mental life. I am not thinking here so much of such splits as that between conscious and unconscious mental entities or of such splits as between the component personalities of a person suffering from multiple personality, for in such cases the divisions normally preclude communication between the entities or personalities that have been split. Thus a person suffering from multiple personality typically is unaware of all of those other selves and may at best be aware of periods of amnesia. Our normal reader, we have seen, on the contrary, gets along quite happily in two different worlds at the same time and is conscious of so doing. Thus while there is a split between Charles screaming and Charles eating his popcorn, Charles himself is aware of both component selves, and presents us with a unity that transcends the division within.

A more helpful analogy with the reader is provided by what is known about the separate consciousnesses of the left and right hemispheres of the brain. For some time it has been recognized that the two halves of our brain experience and can think about the world rather differently, but this difference is masked by the communication that normally occurs between them and that is effected by a bundle of nerve fibers called the *corpus callosum*. This bundle has been severed experimentally in animals and therapeutically in some humans suffering from an otherwise uncontrollable form of epilepsy. Patients whose hemispheres have been thus split do not normally present any very strange behavior, because even though the *corpus callosum* has been severed, their two hemispheres manage to communicate externally, as it were. Their right hands know what their left hands are doing because both hemispheres can literally *see* what they are doing. But it is possible experimentally to prevent such external communication between the brain's two halves. (This can be quite a complex task because, for example, the vision in each of our eyes is split up, half of what one eye sees being transmitted to one hemisphere, half to the other; nonetheless, it is possible to rig up an apparatus such that split-brain patients' left hemispheres, for example, cannot see what their right hemispheres can. And of course objects placed in one hand or the other can easily be screened from vision altogether.) In such experimental setups quite strange things do occur. Thomas Nagel, a philosopher interested in the problem of consciousness, reports what he rightly calls "a particularly poignant example of conflict between the hemispheres":

> A pipe is placed out of sight in the patient's left hand, and he is then asked to write with his left hand what he was holding. Very laboriously and heavily, the left hand writes the letters P and I. Then suddenly the writing speeds up and becomes lighter, the I is converted to an E, and the word is completed as PENCIL. Evidently the left hemisphere has made a guess based on the appearance of the first two letters, and has interfered, with ipsilateral control.

But then the right hemisphere takes over control of the hand again, heavily crosses out the letters ENCIL, and draws a crude picture of a pipe.[58]

We need not concern ourselves with detailed accounts of why things occur in just this way; the point of the analogy is that it suggests ways in which consciousness can be at once divided and unitary. For split-brain patients do not experience themselves as having divided consciousness any more than Charles does. Indeed, the burden of Nagel's argument is finally not about people with split brains but about the conditions of normal consciousness. Nagel sees five possible interpretations of the experimental data, each of which offers an explanation in terms of a certain number of minds that these patients have. But Nagel also offers good reasons for why each of those interpretations is unacceptable. His conclusion therefore is that these people cannot be said to have any *countable whole number* of minds. And he continues: "If I am right, and there is no whole number of individual minds that these patients can be said to have, then the attribution of conscious, significant mental activity does not require the existence of a single mental subject."[59] And this naturally leads Nagel to pose the same question of the normal mind and so entertain

the possibility that our own unity may be nothing absolute, but merely another case of integration, more or less effective, in the control system of a complex organism. This system speaks in the first person singular through our mouths, and that makes it understandable that we should think of its unity as in some sense numerically absolute. . . .

But this is quite genuinely an illusion. The illusion consists in projecting inward to the center of the mind the very subject whose unity we are trying to explain: the individual person with all his complexities. The ultimate account of the unity of what we call a single mind consists of an enumeration of the types of functional integration that typify it. We know that these can be eroded in different ways, and to different degrees. The belief that even in their complete version they can be explained by the presence of a numerically single subject is an illusion. Either this subject contains the mental life, in which case it is complex and its unity must be accounted for in terms of the unified operation of its components and functions, or else it is an extensionless point, in which case it explains nothing.[60]

While such a view justifies our talk about the divisions within a reader, therefore, it ought to make us as skeptical about talk of two or any other whole number of readers (within one reading person) as about talk of a single, unitary reader. In other words, a fact about our reading no less remarkable than the division within us is that we do not experience the division as a rupture within some more normal state. The point, once again, is not about pathological states, but normal ones.

Another analogy drawn from phenomena almost all of us continually experience may help us grasp the normality of the division within reading. Our literal vision of the world is made up, as we all learn as children, of two separate images seen by each eye respectively. Together these images make up binocular, stereoscopic vision. The mysterious thing about stereoscopic vision is that it entails the remarkable ability to see two separate (even if highly similar) images as one. To see stereoscopically, that is, depends upon the ability to fuse two images perceptually in such a way that we no longer see each separately although we are aware, certainly, of each separate image. Each image is in some sense lost in the composite one, and yet none of the information that each conveys is lost, and we are certainly aware of each, though not aware of each except as a part of the composite— otherwise we would suffer *double* vision, the confusing superimposition of two separate images that fail to fuse. What is difficult to understand in all of this is the riddle of how the component images of normal binocular vision can at once be said to be distinguishable and not distinguishable. Although a lot is known about binocular vision, this fundamental riddle remains almost as puzzling today as when it was first noted by the ancient Greeks.[61] To connect the problem with that of the split-brain patient and put it most emphatically, we can pose the problem thus: It is axiomatic that a person cannot be in two places at once. And yet that is precisely what seems to be the case when I view the world stereoscopically. For surely I view the world through my right eye with my whole person just as much as I view it through my left with my whole person. It is not just a piece of my whole self that sees what each eye singly sees, and persons with one eye are surely no less whole persons than those with two. So then my whole person must see the world from two separate positions simultaneously when I view the world with both eyes open and must therefore be in two distinct places at once, for I must be in a place in order to see from its standpoint. As in the case of split-brain patients, the riddle comes about only because of our devotion to the notion of a "whole" person.

Our analogies drawn from the cognitive sciences suggest some ways in which consciousness endures and even consists of divided consciousnesses that are fundamentally in conflict, even in outright contradiction with one another. We can let the scientists and philosophers worry about solutions to these riddles. Our job is rather simply to see how their existence ought to make us suspicious of attempts to make up a theory of fiction that has been purged of contradiction. The existence of fictions is not merely a logically difficult fact, but at bottom a fundamentally paradoxical one. *When we talk about fictions as though we did not believe seriously in them, we are in effect closing one eye no less than when we talk about fictions as though we believed in them.*

The question before us now is how does our discussion of fictional belief together with the model of reading we have developed help us understand the significance of talk about *probability* with respect to fictions.

Chapter VIII

Fictional Probability

IN DISCOVERING the antinomy of fictional probability we discovered a logical oddity that comes about whenever we ascribe degrees of probability to things known never to have existed. This antinomy can be understood, though not done away with, through an analysis of the nature of our belief in fictions, an analysis that turns out to involve an analysis of the nature of fiction itself. In the view of Kendall Walton, fictions are props used in games of make-believe, and to make believe is to adopt a dual standpoint from which sometimes entirely contradictory things may simultaneously be true. When we entertain fictions, we have available to us multiple frames of reference and therefore multiple sets of evidence: the evidence from the "real" world and evidence from the "fictional" world. It is the fact of a gap between these standpoints or worlds that makes possible the invocation of standards of literary probability. Precisely because I *pretend* that something fictional is real, there is opened up the possibility of my ascribing probability to it.

That the logic of fictions allows readers to talk about the probability of fictions does not explain why readers have actually talked about them and talked about them at such length. In order to understand the significance of talk about the probability of fictions, we need to understand the peculiar interest of such talk to readers, and to do that we have to consider readers more developed than Charles, for example. For while Charles can show us things that go on in all people as they entertain fictions, he obviously is not the sort to ascribe probability to the green slime.

Let us consider a somewhat more grown-up reader; indeed, let us imagine ourselves as we read for example a classic work of fiction like Conrad's "Heart of Darkness." Being absorbed by the tale—that is, being in an active state of making believe—we can say it is true of this reader that he at once believes in Mr. Kurtz and does not. His believing in Mr. Kurtz is a lot like the believing that Buonamici's madman would engage in, for our reader is willing to follow Marlow's lead, willing to take Marlow's account of Kurtz as authoritative; when Marlow writes, "I could see the cage of his ribs all astir, the bones of his arms waving,"[1] our absorbed reader takes Marlow's claim and his description at their word, imagines Kurtz gesturing thus, probably imagines what Kurtz "must" have looked like to produce such a description. Our reader's simultaneously disbelieving in Kurtz is, all the same, a lot like the disbelief of one who refuses to play the game of pretend at all. The absorbed reader knows Kurtz is "merely" fictional, knows that Kurtz exists "in fact" only as some black marks on the pages of books, exists in fact only in language. He also believes in the literal existence of some things incompatible with Kurtz's existence, and in holding these beliefs he is utterly unlike Buonamici's madman or imbecile and quite like the reader who refuses to pretend. Among the real objects of such beliefs are such things perhaps as the chairs and rooms in which we read as well as the historical person Joseph Conrad, the community of readers of English literature (who know "Heart of Darkness" is fiction), and so on. He is just as much a believer in these objects as the reader who refuses to pretend. So far so good: these beliefs and disbeliefs are already familiar to us from our discussions of literary belief. But consider now the *general* beliefs that our reader may hold about the world, beliefs on the order of "killing people is wrong" or "human nature is at bottom ugly" or "the people involved in the colonial exploitation of the Belgian Congo were by and large good examples of the banality of evil." These beliefs about the real world have an obvious relevance to our absorbed reader's experience of the tale: they at once constitute a background against which the tale is read and constitute a field of beliefs that may itself be altered by a reading of the tale.[2] And in this latter aspect they present us with something quite new to our discussion, for thus far we have been concerned about beliefs in a reader that appear contradictory, but that have in fact no power to alter one another, precisely because they inhabit separate worlds. But when it comes to such complex and general beliefs as that "human nature is at bottom ugly," it would seem that here at last some quite literal contact between real and fictional worlds is not only possible but inevitable. To borrow an example from M. H. Abrams, thus far we have been concerned about the reader's beliefs in such assertions as, "It is an ancient Mariner,/And he stoppeth one of three," whereas now we need to worry also about such assertions as, "He prayeth best, who loveth best,/All things both great and small."[3] And in particular we have to worry about the tensions between beliefs in these two sorts of assertion.

By pretending that the fiction we read is real, it seems to me that we obviously allow for two things. The first is the possibility of a temporary suspension of a many of our general beliefs, a suspension that is part of the game of pretend. The second is the possibility of a change in the general beliefs with which we came to the text. By pretending that the literal truth that a fiction asserts is true, I may come to be really (that is, literally, non-make-believedly) persuaded that a general truth it asserts is true as well. The latter possibility is of course a necessary implication of any general theory of fictions ("literary" or otherwise) that claims fictions have the power to teach us anything, which theory would itself seem to follow from any view of fictions as being more than mindless entertainments. The beliefs a reader has about killing, about how deep civilization extends into human character, about the ethics of colonialism, and so forth, are all liable to change through a reading of "Heart of Darkness." If the reader is a very credulous one, those changes may occur through some real confusion about the literal reality of Marlow, but if the reader is at all sophisticated about the fictions, those changes will occur in spite of the reader's knowing perfectly well that there never really was a Marlow or a Kurtz. And in this aspect the sophisticated reader is now quite unlike either Buonamici's madman or the reader who refuses to pretend. (Recall that up to this point we have been able to show that he shares various attributes of these two extreme types; what distinguished him from them is how these attributes are combined at the time he is reading.) The madman and imbecile in our model passively accept whatever they are told; the reader who refuses to pretend accepts nothing. But our more usual reader is engaged in a far more complicated game of give-and-take with the text he reads.

We can see this most clearly if we introduce another dimension to the discussion and look at the reader through time, not only as he reads through the text itself, but as he continues to think about it through several readings and indeed even when he is not actually reading it at all. There is for this reader an inevitable tension between the field of his own general beliefs that have some bearing on the text and the field of beliefs that is generated by the text. This tension puts to the text a constant challenge to continue to be persuasive or "believable." Therefore our reader is now not simply to be described as an absorbed reader, but as a reader who is sometimes absorbed and sometimes not. For, after all, the reader's belief in the fiction is not a one-time thing. It is not that the reader at some point ceases to believe in Marlow and then suddenly comes to believe in him. Rather he moves in and out of the game of pretend, sometimes (especially if he is a sober critic) behaving very much like the one who refuses to pretend, sometimes behaving like quite a credulous reader indeed, and perhaps sometimes behaving like a reader who simultaneously is and is not pretending (as opposed to the merely pretending reader who behaves simultaneously like a believer and a nonbeliever).[4]

There are of course countless factors determining our degree of imaginative involvement with any given text at any given time, but here our interest is simply with the fact of different intensities of pretending. We can perhaps most readily see the movement into pretending by recalling our own experience of "getting into" a particular work of fiction for the first time and then getting out of it again. Especially if the author is new to us, we often have to work hard through many pages before we are "into it" and fully absorbed by the game of pretend. It is not that for those first pages we refuse to pretend altogether, but our involvement in the game is less profound and our experience of the fiction less vivid than it will be when we are fully absorbed by it. We may find we have actively and consciously to *work* at pretending. We may even find that our comprehension and retention of the narrative are not strong because we are not entirely engaged in it. The critic in us is likely to be working hard through these initial pages, perhaps overworking, so that we are not only divided selves (as all engaged in games of make-believe must be), but even uncomfortably aware of the division and aware of our not having entirely let ourselves go imaginatively. Once we are fully into a text, the critic will become relatively silent and even our awareness of our immediate surroundings dims. This doesn't mean we fail to get along in the real world any longer, but we may miss the popcorn box or even forget it altogether. If the extent of our pretending has been very great—if in other words we really have been gripped by the fiction—the reappearance of the critic may be felt only after the book has been put down. But it is more usual for us to experience, especially with longer works repeated moves in and out of the game of pretend. When the book is at last finished, the critic may not have found much to object to and we may count ourselves among the true believers in the author's work. But then again doubts may arise that lead us to question our willingness to play the author's game so deeply, and we may be inspired therefore to reread and to test our own first impressions. We are now quite adept at entering this particular imaginative world, but also in a sense quite adept at staying out of it. It is difficult or impossible to recapture the absorption of a first reading. So we may believe or pretend quite intensely in some ways even as the critic in us doubts and questions. For example, our first reaction to Kurtz's, "The horror! The horror!" may have been strong and appropriately full of our own sense of horror. Perhaps after we have thought about things for a while and reread the text over a number of years, the horror loses some or much of its edge. We do not, let us say, cease to believe in Kurtz (cease to pretend Kurtz was a real fellow), but perhaps we cease to believe in him as so appropriate an emblem of an aspect of our own human predicament. We may ask ourselves, "After all that *we* have seen, was Kurtz's experience really so horrible after all?" Or perhaps, to imagine quite a different reaction, Kurtz becomes for us *so* appropriate an emblem of the human predicament that we gradually invest him with a number of attributes hard to substantiate in the text. Perhaps we forget much about his particularity and begin to think of him as rather more like ourselves. In both of these quite different cases, the reader in important respects has ceased to play the game, or has become at least a less faithful player, though perhaps without ever quite realizing it.

This sketch of a reader's relationship with a particular text is not of course meant to convey details important to our experience of reading, but only to remind us of the vicissitudes of our pretending as we pass from first-time to *n*th-time readers of a fiction. At any given moment when we are reading or reflecting upon the fiction, the state of our pretending will be in flux. This does not necessarily mean that there is a question for example about whether we are making believe that Marlow and Kurtz are real fellows, however; for probably throughout all our readings of and reflections about "Heart of Darkness" we agree to treat them as make-believedly true (except perhaps when we feel the need to remind ourselves that they are merely fictional beings who exist only as marks on a page—but those moments are I suggest rare even among sober critics who like to point to fiction's fictionality). But it does mean on the one hand that our belief in their significance and relevance may be continually changing and in doubt and that on the other hand they have (or their stories have) at any moment the power to alter any of our general beliefs about the world that we can see as having some relevance to their stories. While we pretend that they are real, there is no real tension between our belief in them and our disbelief in them or between our belief in them and our belief in, for example, our chairs. The tension there is only apparent, as Walton has shown, and, again, appears only to the extent that we fail to take seriously the duality of the make-believer's standpoint. From the perspective of these beliefs there is no real tension therefore between the real and fictional worlds. But between the more general beliefs about the world that a fiction either assumes or seeks to persuade a reader of and the general beliefs about the world that a reader brings to a text, there is potentially plainly a real tension, and from the perspective of *these* beliefs there is potentially a real tension between the real and fictional worlds. This real tension does not mean that Kendall Walton's analysis about the impossibility of contact between real and fictional worlds is in its own terms wrong, and one could at this point make the objection in the light of that analysis that we have been talking as though the general beliefs about the world implied or generated by a fiction themselves belong to the real world and therefore could have contact with a reader's beliefs, whereas in fact these beliefs are fictionally generated and belong entirely to the fictional world. But if it is necessarily fictional that there exists Mr. Pickwick, it is not necessarily fictional that benevolence is a virtue or that Mr. Pickwick's character is comical. If we want to say that *The Pickwick Papers* generates these latter fictions, they are nonetheless distinct from the former in that they may be seriously, non-make-believedly true or treated as true. In that sense they can enter the real world (be nonfictional) in a way that the former cannot.

In the domain of general beliefs about the world, therefore, fictional and real worlds do in this sense really meet after all, and the sign of that meeting is the reader's emergence from the fictional world a somewhat different person—that is, a person with a somewhat different set of general beliefs. This is not the place to examine what kinds of change are actually wrought through our contact with fictional worlds. That obviously is today a controversial question, one that many literary theorists and critics prefer not to touch in particular detail at all (at least without some neutralizing move—such as translating "belief" into "ideology"). Sociologists, legislators, and others worry about such practical concerns as, for instance, how violence on TV may affect children adversely—that is, foster a general belief among them that violence is alright. And professors of literature rightly caution against simplistic arguments that we are what we read or watch or listen to. But I take it for granted that even the soberest of us believe that effects of some kind there are, and that these effects alter in some fashion our general beliefs about things.

Readers are of course not instructed by fictions in the sense of simply incorporating the lessons of fictions. It is just this fact that may make us nervous of talk about what lessons fictions actually may teach. In this domain in which fictional worlds really do touch us who are inhabitants of the real world, we touch and change the fictions as well—not, to be sure, in the sense in which we imagined that a credulous playgoer might change the fiction of a play by leaping onto the stage and preventing a villain from doing in the heroine or by forcing the playwright at gunpoint to alter the script. Insofar as we agree to let the fiction have some objective status, as it is for example manifested in a text, we agree to try to arrive at a version of the text that is definitive and that will endure pretty much unchanged. But insofar as the fiction actually becomes a model for our private instruction and use, insofar as it is a prop in our private game of make-believe, it is subject to quite considerable revision, as we have already supposed in imagining how time might alter our reading of "Heart of Darkness." All of those difficult philosophical questions that make us wonder what sort of communication is possible at all of course suggest that our experience of a fiction must be different from everyone else's, but, in addition, the fact that we obviously do not incorporate fictional models whole into our own models of the world means that at the very least we abridge them. If the previous example of various ways in which we might come to think about Kurtz has plausibility, then we must do quite a bit of more obviously active rewriting as well. The evidence of the text generates fictional truths of a more or less general kind. As the more general of these interact with the more general beliefs with which we come to the text, our apprehension of the evidence of the text may itself shift. Depending upon the general truths that Kurtz's story seems to us to embody, and depending upon how we would let these modify our general beliefs about the world, we shall feature certain particularities of Kurtz more or less prominently in our view of him. Some particularities we may forget, exclude, or repress altogether; others we may simply alter; others we may invent through inference. And of course it is not just the particularities of character that we treat thus. *Any* detail of the text is liable to our rewriting it unawares.

The rewriting of fictions that I am talking about goes on even among sober critics who are perfectly aware that the canons of good criticism have for a couple of hundred of years now frowned upon doing such violence to a text. Criticism among a community would not seem to be possible at all if we are free to alter the objects of our criticism at will, which is a good reason for having canons against rewriting texts and for asserting the objectivity of texts. But rewriting texts is plainly inevitable. No doubt the sober critic feels superior to the hapless freshman who in arguing for his own reading evidently has forgotten important details of a text or who in attacking another's reading blurts out, "I don't believe Kurtz would ever have done that anyway," but the superiority lies in the sober critic's ability to play the same game of rewriting less obtrusively. The successful critic must indeed appear to be in complete command of the evidence of the text, must appear to take into account all the evidence, and must hide the fact of his own rewriting skillfully. But rewrite and alter he does, which is after all what prevents any particular reading from being definitive and therefore what fortunately allows the game of criticism to go on. The successful critic is the one who persuades us that his account of *his* private game of make-believe is in fact an account of *our* private game as well. Or the successful critic persuades us rather that it is an account of no private game at all, but rather what ought to be a public one. The successful critic succeeds, in other words, in making his private account a public one. The evidence of the text is always available to give the publicality of the game credibility, but the fact that we agree upon the prop to be used in the game of make-believe in itself does not guarantee that everyone is going to play the same game and so make believe the same things.

We have hedged in discussing the kinds of general beliefs about the world that might be relevant to particular fictions by imagining purposely vague beliefs (such as that "human nature is at bottom ugly"). In part this is precisely to avoid the impression that there is anything very clear-cut in *what* fictions have to teach us, but in part too it is to avoid the related impression that fiction's lessons (be they clear-cut themselves or not) are learnt in some hard and fast way (as though once we had learned that "human nature is at bottom ugly" the question could be put behind us forevermore). Both the content of our beliefs and the definiteness with which they are learned and then held are a good deal fuzzier than we would like to imagine. Although we may in fact at a certain moment in our reading (or reflecting) say something like, "The lesson of Kurtz's life is that human nature is at bottom ugly," we are likely to recognize even in so vague a formulation something too sweeping and too definite (as well as banal). And so we will more likely say something like, "Yes, it really is as Conrad says," which is just the response that realist fiction in particular hopes for. This is an interesting way to express the fuzziness of our beliefs, because while from one point of view it is very vague indeed, from another it is not vague at all; it asserts the truth of Conrad's tale and apparently returns us to the game of pretend. In fact such a thought is really quite ambiguous: Does "it" refer us back to all the particularities of the tale or only to the general view of things that the tale may be said to embody or generate? Such an expression in other words asserts that the tale is one from which we may draw a lesson, but at the same time evidently prefers not to draw any particular lesson. To say that we feel there are lessons to be drawn I think is to say no more than that interpretation is possible; to say that we are reluctant actually to draw the lessons I think is to say that we want to avoid reductions— interpretations that can replace their own objects. And here again the reader attempts and perhaps succeeds in having it both ways: in asserting there is a lesson to be learned, he registers the tension between his beliefs about the world and those he perceives the text is attempting to persuade him of, but in not making the lesson explicit, the reader avoids resolving that very tension. Instead of passing from one state of belief to another, which would be the usual course we follow in learning a lesson, the reader allows the text rather to define a field of play, an area of uncertainty.

What is it that keeps this tension and so the sense of uncertainty alive? It is not simply our persistence in playing the game of make-believe, even though that requires us to take what we perfectly well know to be fictional as perfectly serious at the same time. For insofar as we take the fiction seriously there is no tension, because we believe the fiction, and insofar as we take the fiction as fiction there is no tension because we do not believe the fiction. (It is from this standpoint that Walton's analysis of make-believe is I think correct in asserting that there is no connection possible between real and fictional worlds.) What keeps the tension alive, rather, is our tendency to move in and out of the game of make-believe, the fact that we play the game self-consciously, and the fact that sometimes we only pretend to pretend. For it is in this movement in and out of the game of make-believe that the boundaries between the real and the fictional break down and we, as we might say, seriously ask ourselves the questions "Is this like the world?" or "Is the world like this?" And in moving in and out of the game of make-believe the tension is in itself in continual flux. We continually reduce and increase the tension by moving now toward resisting the lesson and now toward drawing it, just as we continually move imaginatively in and out of the fiction itself. And it is here that probability turns out to be an interesting and useful concept in dealing with and understanding that tension and uncertainty.

Recall that we were led to consider the whole question of literary belief because the idea of probability cannot ultimately be considered apart from a consideration of belief and because discussions of literary probability have sometimes (and rightly, if somewhat circularly) assumed considerations of literary probability to be considerations about literary belief. Recall too that we found something logically very strange about applying probability to fictions even though Aristotle, who launches the modern tradition of thinking about probability among both philosophers and literary theorists, evidently approves just that and even though his practice continues throughout the history of literary theory and criticism. The strangeness—what I have called the antinomy of fictional probability—arises from the consideration that it makes sense to think probabilistically only when questions of actual fact are in question. As make-believers who are aware of the real world and competent to get along in it, we are perfectly certain that no Mr. Kurtz ever existed, so what sense could it make to talk about his probability? And even if we go on to adopt the make-believer's standpoint from which he does (in pretend) believe in Kurtz, it remains logically strange to speak of his probability, for from this standpoint too nothing really is in doubt. If I pretend that Kurtz and Marlow are real, then I must follow the lead of the evidence of the text and take their existences as certain. Indeed, while the rules of fiction-reading allow me to question some aspects of the tale (in that Marlow may turn out to be an unreliable narrator), in fact I have only the evidence of this text to go on, and in that sense the evidence of the text is absolute and definitive. Any inferences I draw about Marlow's reliability have to be drawn exclusively from the text of the tale itself. If probabilistic considerations enter here they do so only as helping us toward interpretations of (or drawing lessons from) the text, not as settling questions about the imagined facts the text depicts. And even if probabilistic thinking helps us with our interpretations, it remains logically strange because we are still dealing with interpretations of "facts" known to be false.

If it is logically absurd to speak of the probabilities of Mr. Kurtz both from the standpoint from which I, as a sane inhabitant of the real world, seriously and entirely disbelieve in the existence of Mr. Kurtz *and* from the standpoint from which I as a good make-believer non-seriously but entirely believe in Mr. Kurtz, then it would seem that if I *do* say something like, "Kurtz's behavior is most improbable," I am somehow forgetting *both* standpoints because from neither do such statements make sense. But how can this be? If it is characteristic for us to overlook the dual standpoint of the make-believer, surely that means that it is characteristic for us to adopt *one* standpoint at the expense of the other (and perhaps be enconscious of our move from one to the other). And if this is so, then it seems odd that talk about probabilities in regard to fictions should ever have come about. From what imaginable standpoint can it be said that we occupy *neither* of the standpoints of the make-believer? To answer this is to answer the question, From what standpoint then does talk about Kurtz's probability make sense?

The answer, I would suggest, is the standpoint in which we actively are moving in and out of the game of make-believe, the standpoint in which we become a certain kind of doubter. It is not quite the standpoint from which we seek to decide whether to be make-believers·or not, for to ask ourselves the question "Shall I (make) believe?" or the question "Shall I disbelieve the fiction?" is already to put ourselves on one side or the other. To speak of probabilities in regard to fictions means that in one sense we already grant *some* reality to the fiction even as that reality is being questioned. We must therefore occupy the dual standpoint of the make-believer even as we apparently "forget" each component of that standpoint. But this is different again from the (dual) standpoint of the usual make-believer because the make-believer fully engaged with the fiction does not "forget" each of his standpoints; he keeps them in various ways separate and distinct. In terms of the analogy with binocular vision, they are fused but not confused. The literary probabilist, on the other hand, in a special way does confuse the standpoint. In one particular way he actually does behave like Buonamici's madman and apparently takes the fiction as seriously, non-make-believedly real, and his talk about probability is in fact the sign of this. For only if the facts depicted in fictions were potentially seriously, non-make-believedly real—only if real questions of fact were in doubt—would it make any sense to ascribe probability to them. The literary probabilist doubts fictions in a way that at the same time permits him to accept the possibility of their truth perhaps as no simple make-believer can, for the simple make-believer at once believes and disbelieves without behaving as though there were any real doubt about the matter; the literary probabilist behaves (that is, speaks or writes) as though there were a real doubt about the matter.

Instead of being simply dual, the standpoint of the literary probabilist is intermediate; it falls *between* standpoints even though it may pretend on occasion to occupy particular standpoints. It is dynamic and unstable. (Douglas Patey discusses a very similar sort of instability in the Augustan theory of literary probability, an instability that in his view had major consequences for subsequent literary theory.)[5] It is owing to this intermediateness that the literary probabilist apparently forgets the two standpoints of the simple make-believer. Difficult as it is to pin down, the intermediacy of the literary probabilist is important to understand for one thing because it belongs to the one person, among all the readers we have been imagining, of whose existence we can be pretty certain. The complete skeptic who refuses to pretend, like the simple make-believer and Buonamici's madman, is clearly an ideal type. I have met critics who claim never to pretend, but the fact that they on occasion speak as though they pretend makes me seriously doubt whether they are actually capable of withholding their power of make-believe. And even in Buonamici's madman there are vestiges of the ability to move in two worlds at once, even if that ability is defective. The psychotic young man whom I have already described as confusing the events in medieval romances with those in the real world, nevertheless managed to deal with the real world sufficiently well to get to class, to open his book and read it, and so on. And while we might seem to have a real instance of the simple make-believer in a young child or even a deeply engrossed adult, it is hard to see how such a make-believer could enter that simple state of make-believe all at once, as it were. Even if there do exist relatively pure states of make-believe, in other words, surely they can be attained only by degrees, so that on the way to the dual standpoint of the make-believer there must occur all sorts of transitional states. I cannot be sure about the extremes of credulity and skepticism or of pure make-believe, therefore, but I can be sure about the intermediate stages, stages about which in my view we have excellent evidence in talk about literary probability.

It is helpful to compare how probabilistic considerations play a part in the game of reading fictions with how they play a part in leading us to form opinions about questions of actual fact. If I want to know something about the real world, my job is to amass as much evidence as I can. At each stage probabilistic thinking should help me to know how much weight to give each piece of evidence and so eventually should lead me to form some opinion on the question, one that itself takes a probabilistic form—even if a relatively imprecise one. Of course the question will remain open, and my opinion will only be as good as the evidence I have at hand (as well as the wisdom with which I decide how to weigh it). New evidence will necessarily affect my opinion. In such a situation, each bit of evidence is added to the pile and figures into what is no doubt a complicated and imprecise sort of calculation. Although I may get lucky and find something out that really appears to settle the question once and for all, nevertheless the evidence I might accumulate on the question is in theory infinite insofar as I can always imagine adding some other "fact" to the pile. Moreover, the evidence I collect is not restricted to the particular question I may have chosen at a certain point to ponder, but can be applied to a theoretically infinite set of other questions upon which the evidence (or some of it) touches. It is continuous (of a piece) with that larger pile of evidence I call my accumulated knowledge and experience of life in that the probabilities I use to assess each piece of evidence I want to apply to a given question are themselves the product of that larger pile of accumulated evidence. The situation, as we have seen, is however quite different when it comes to playing the game of reading and judging fictions. Instead of being faced with an infinite amount of evidence and an infinite number of facts that can at best be agreed upon as highly probable, the reader of fictions is faced with a closed body of evidence (provided by the text) and a closed body of facts, many of which can be agreed upon as certain. Whereas in the real world everything may be doubted, including everything we consider evidence, in the world of fiction the one thing that cannot in practice be doubted is the evidence of the text itself. Because some fictional facts are in this sense unquestionable and because the facts of any particular fiction are finite, it is impermissible to ask many questions of fictions that are permissible in the real world—like the question of how many children had Mr. Pickwick. The closed body of evidence provided in any fiction is also logically separate from the accumulated evidence I call my knowledge and experience in that I cannot make it relevant to the real world simply by adding it to the larger pile. Surely I am not actually permitted to infer from Kurtz's behavior something about human nature in general, or even about colonial agents in particular, simply because it is all (in terms of serious facts about the real world) a lie. But if there is to be any game of make-believe that is more than a mindless escape or a mindless reflection of what I already believe, something has got to give: the two piles of evidence must communicate in some way, "impermissible" though that may be. And as we have been assuming, of course, we do just such an impermissible thing as inferring things about the real world from fictional worlds when we let the fiction teach us something (even if the lesson is baseless, which is another question).

It is probability that makes this communication possible (even if it remains logically impermissible) and that mediates between the real and fictional worlds, without simply eradicating the distinction between them and therefore without entirely ignoring the impermissibility of that communication. Our sense of what is probable provides the means by which the tension between the evidence of reality and the evidence of fictions is tested and maintained. To revert to our analogy between reading and binocular vision, we could say that probabilistic judgment is the counterpart of the faculty that fuses distinct images. It is what surveys and bridges the gap between what we believe about the world and what a fiction asks us to believe. In this sense probability *can* be said to provide a standard against which fictions may be judged, as is implicit from the very beginning of discussions of literary probability in Aristotle.

But again this does not mean that we have in any way resolved the problem of the antinomy of fictional probability or made the use of a probabilistic standard a logical thing. We have made sense of fictional probability through our understanding of the duality and dynamics of the make-believer's standpoint. Our account does mean that, thanks to our analysis of fictional belief, we can give a somewhat better account of fictional probability than is embodied in what we have called the "commonsensical" answer to the question of how questions of probability arise among readers of fictions. Remember that the "commonsensical" account said talk about fictional probability is merely the sign that a fiction is an imitation of the real and that someone is treating a fiction as real. Someone actually treating a fiction as real of course would behave like Buonamici's madman and someone treating a fiction as *probably* or *possibly* real would behave like a sober scholar and look for corroborating evidence elsewhere. The literary probabilist, in contrast, treats the fiction as just what we have seen Kendall Walton define it as being, a prop in a game of make-believe. That is, he treats the text at once as true and not true, he adopts a dual standpoint relative to it, and he has it both ways. But he does, as we have seen, something more than simply pretend. By invoking probabilities, he has cast himself in the role of the doubter. He not only splits himself up by adopting two perspectives, but he in a sense hovers between them insofar as his manner of speaking at once extends and withholds belief.

This picture of the literary probabilist should help us see, moreover, not only why talk about fictional probability should *arise*, but why the logic of probability should be much more prominent among critics of fictions than among historians, and why it should *persist*. For if talk about probability is generated by the movement in and out of the game of make-believe that reading fiction consists of, it should be clear that talk about probability is something that the reader of fictions can never really get *beyond*. When questions of real fact are in doubt, as they are among historians, than probability is a guide that helps us to come to some opinion on the question at hand. When no questions of fact are actually in doubt, there are no real questions finally to be decided, no final opinions to be arrived at. In the real world, new evidence is necessarily piled upon old, but in the game of fiction the evidence of the real world and the evidence of fictional worlds necessarily remain separate and continually in tension, and so to play the game is to keep alive that tension of which talk about probability is the sign. I can only cease to doubt by blindly assenting to the fiction or by complete withdrawing from its world, in both of which cases the game is over.

We are at last in a position, then, to say in some detail what is the general significance of sentences like, "Kurtz's behavior is probable," or, "Kurtz's behavior is improbable." Let us take the positive case first. It means most importantly that the reader is a make-believer, but it is a sign of more than just that. It is a sign of the make-believer's dual standpoint insofar as it registers a degree of belief and a degree of disbelief at the same time. It says, "I am willing to play the game," but it says in addition, "I am not willing to do so slavishly. I may withhold my belief and withdraw from the game, though at the moment I'm inclined to keep playing." Thus it asserts neither simply that I accept the fiction (accept these assertions as make-believedly true) nor simply that I refuse to accept the fiction as really false. And in this sense it negates the dual standpoints of the make-believer. By assuming the position of a doubter, one who assents to the possibility of the game but who reserves the right to reject the fiction in part, the literary probabilist asserts a new fiction—his own—above and beyond the one he is engaged in reading. By entering the game of make-believe at all, of course, one begins one's own game. But in addition the literary probabilist says not merely that "I pretend that Kurtz is real (and so go along with the author's game)," but "I pretend to pretend that Kurtz is real (and so have *my own* game)." Where Conrad, we have said, actually asserts that Kurtz is make-believedly real, the reader may in addition make-believedly assert that Kurtz is make-believedly real. In pretending to pretend, the probabilistic reader asserts a degree of control over the fiction that the simple make-believer does not, and one aspect of this control is the literary probabilist's power to revise the original fiction. It is this fact too that is registered in his ascriptions of probability to a fiction. This is most apparent if we turn to the negative case, the sentence "Kurtz's behavior is improbable." To say a fictional being's actions are *im*probable is to assert that one is moving out of the game of pretend, away from make-believe. Like the positive case, it registers both the reader's dual standpoint and a forgetting of each of those standpoints. The negative case says, "I am willing to play the game, but at the moment I'm inclined not to, because somehow the evidence doesn't add up." Because the evidence of the text seems inconsistent in itself or because it seems inconsistent with what the reader believes beyond the text (and has no reason to suspect he has been asked to disbelieve), the reader rewrites the text—by rejecting some part of it.[6] And yet even here the literary probabilist avoids making his rewriting of the text entirely public. He is not so bold and unsocial as to say, "It didn't happen that way at all; *I* know how Kurtz actually behaved," nor is he even so bold as to say, "I don't believe this account of Kurtz's behavior." There is in his ascribing mere improbability to Kurtz's behavior the possibility that he is saying simply, "I am prepared to accept the evidence of the text's account of how Kurtz behaved, and yet I have to say there is evidence (from the text, from

the real world) to show that something is not right with that account."
And yet here too a rewriting of sorts is going on, for this is to raise the
(fictional) possibility that the evidence we have (from the text, from the
real world) is not sufficient to make for a (fictionally) probable account.
There must (fictionally) be some additional evidence that would make
it probable that Kurtz behaved as described. This additional evidence
can of course only be of the reader's imaginative devising and is a part
therefore of the reader's contribution to the fiction.

It is tempting in looking at these cases to assume that the important
thing is the direction in which each reader is headed: the speaker of the
positive case toward belief, the speaker of the negative case toward
disbelief. But I want to insist on what these two readers have in common, that they are both speaking from positions in movement and in
transition, and that each is in some proper way playing the game of
reading fiction. When we object to their talk about probability because
it overlooks the evidence of the text as given and which is not to be
questioned, we object from a standpoint outside the game of make-
believe. And this is true not only if we say, "You can't talk about the
probability of Kurtz because Kurtz is in fact fictional and therefore has
zero probability—that is, no probability at all"; it is no less true if we
say, "You must believe in Kurtz as he is described, for the game
requires you to believe, requires you to take the evidence of the text as
final, requires that you not rewrite it, requires that you ascribe to Kurtz
a probability of one—that is, no probability at all, but certainty."
Make-believers, we have seen, can take neither position, but must take
both. They have it both ways *and have to* have it both ways. This
contradiction shows us the full force of the antinomy of fictional
probability.

There is one final and very important aspect of talk about the
probability of fictions that is implicit in our account. It is that talk
about the probability of fictions is peculiarly useful in public discussions
about fictions. This follows precisely from the literary probabilist's
intermediate position at once in and outside the game of make-believe,
at once believing and doubting. If on the one hand we accept a fiction

wholly and slavishly, we are not left with much to say except by way of celebration. This of course is a fine thing to do in the company of other celebrants. A certain amount of organized literary activity has just this function, but it does not do much to advance our understanding of literature in itself. If on the other hand we refuse to accept a fiction at all, then it would also seem that we can have nothing to say about it at all. Many writers throughout history have of course pointed to the fictionality of fictions, but this is far from entirely refusing to play the game of make-believe. One can merely pretend *not* to pretend. I know of no criticism in which sentences like, "Don Quixote was crazy," are *always* merely elliptical for, "In the novel *Don Quixote*, the protagonist was crazy," but even if there be such criticism, its existence does not disprove my point, for to say something so self-conscious and distancing as, "The nonexistent fictional character was make-believedly crazy," still is to assume that we all know how to pretend and that we all know what is being pretended. It is hard to imagine, however, how one could convey the sense of such a sentence to a being who lacked the faculty of make-believe altogether. But to adopt the intermediate, doubting standpoint of the literary probabilist is not only to say to the fiction, "You may have something to teach me," it is to say to anyone who adopts the same stance, "We may have something to teach one another." It is to invite the comparison of evidence not just between one reader's experience of the world and that of the text, but between any number of reader's experiences of world and a text. To ascribe probability to a fiction is also to allow for degrees of probability among various readings of that fiction—something one cannot do either if one is a simple make-believer (and celebrant) or if one refuses to play the game at all, for in the one case there is no "reading" necessary; there is only the supreme authority of the text, and in the other there is nothing real to be read. Once again we may question whether these extreme types themselves are real: celebrants in fact are peculiarly liable to discover errors in one another's celebrations, and the volubility of those who pretend that they do not pretend I think itself suggests they know very well how to play the game; it is not just that they protest too much; it is that they protest at all. But if the extremes are merely ideal, that is only to say that in fact we all really do take up the position of literary probabilists and thus all put ourselves in a position to adapt our private games to make-believe to a larger, public one conducted by criticism.

Conclusion

Probability, Play, and the Novel

IN ADDITION to some speculative questions about the future of the theory of fictions, a couple of large practical questions remain to be answered. The first concerns our historical understanding of fiction in the modern period and how our analysis might inform it, and the second concerns the consequences for criticism of the analysis we have conducted.

Our first large question is to ask what our argument can add to a historical understanding of the origins of the novel: How might one revise the story we tell about the origins of the modern novel based upon this discussion of literary probability? Here the consequences of our analysis are fortunate ones, I think, for my argument has covered much that can usefully be added to our knowledge of what, since Ian Watt's classic account of it, has come to be called "the rise of the novel."

At the outset of this book I tried to forestall criticism that the view I have taken is not sufficiently historical by noting that my interests have not been in *what* particular periods have found probable or improbable in fictions, but *that* critics have found anything in fictions probable at all, from Aristotle to the present. We have not been as interested in particular logics governing literary probability at any one time within that larger period—logics outlining the rules of probabilistic inference in literature such as Douglas Patey has exposited among the Augustans, for example—so much as in the more general logic that makes literary probability possible. But of course there are interdependencies between the questions of the "what" and the "that" of probability, and we may profitably if briefly consider how what we have argued here might accord with our understanding of the birth of the novel.

That understanding still largely derives from Ian Watt's *The Rise of the Novel*, a book that lots of writers have argued against on one point or another, but that continues to give the account that all others must contend with of what is surely the most dramatic development in the literary history of the last several hundred years.[1] Like Hacking's argument about the emergence of probability, it can be assailed from many standpoints, but it survives as a classic because it raises all the right questions, at least concerning the English tradition of the novel.[2] Watt was the first to assemble most of the important elements that must go into any recipe for the modern novel. Most centrally and broadly, those elements are the coming into power of the middle class and the growing interest among philosophers and ordinary people alike in the particularities of individual experience. Along with the rise of the middle class, there comes into being a new audience of readers with both the leisure and access to books necessary to read fiction (an audience including substantial numbers of women, apprentices, and household servants), a growing business in the production and circulation of books, the emergence of new standards of credibility in the evidence available to historians and the law courts, and the development of new forms of writing and publishing (e.g., journalism in the form both of periodicals specializing in essays and of newspapers; diaries; books of letters, books of travel, and so on) that provide fiction writers with new techniques for both the invention and dissemination of their works.

These elements together produce what Watt considers to be the definitive technique of the novel, what he calls its "formal realism"—

> the premise, or primary convention, that the novel is a full and
> authentic report of human experience, and is therefore under an
> obligation to satisfy its reader with such details of the story as the
> individuality of the actors concerned, the particulars of the times
> and places of their actions, details which are presented through a

more largely referential use of language than is common in other literary forms.[3]

It is on this question of realism that Watt's account is of course most vulnerable, for while he is aware that formal realism is, as he says, "like the rules of evidence, *only* a convention" (my emphasis), nevertheless he himself writes very much within a realist tradition that generally eclipses that awareness behind its own faith in the accuracy of the representation.[4] And even though he is himself very helpful about the history of realism in reminding us that it is basically a mid-nineteenth-century invention, nevertheless that awareness too is often eclipsed.[5]

Writing within a tradition of realism, Watt shares also with the mid-nineteenth century a view of the eighteenth century as an age quite confident in its faith in reason and its own power to know things about the world through the certainty of the senses. But that view does not accord very well with the novel's concern from early on with all the obstacles that stand in the way of knowing. Although it is fair to characterize the novel as anxious to see as much of reality as possible, the anxiety is made poignant precisely by the novel's sensitivity to the precariousness of the project. The form is not very old before writers like Sterne and Austen have made appearance and illusion no less powerful and determining than the real. But in any case, from its very beginnings, the reality that the novel has depicted has hardly been a model of the predictable working of reason. To no small degree, that is of course why novels are interesting.

Bringing probability into the center of things, in favor of reality and realism, makes for a better account precisely because the novel identifies a problem in our apprehension of reality. Bringing probability to the center emphasizes doubt and uncertainty—the obstacles so minutely explored by the novel that stand between us and certain knowledge. But to claim that the novel is the product of a probabilistic age is not to write an antirealist account of the birth of the novel, for to invoke probability is hardly to deny the presence of reality or the urgency of recognizing that presence; it is rather to deny that reality can be certainly known. Our claim therefore leaves much more of Watt's account intact than would studies with strongly antirealist sentiments —studies that delight in exposing fiction's fictionality, that is.[6]

Can it be coincidental that the modern novel is born when discussion of literary probability is at its peak? Or can it be coincidental that the concept of probability that makes the mathematical theory of probability possible comes into being only thirty years or so before Defoe launches the modern novel in England? Is there something to do with probability going on in the realm of philosophy, in other words, that makes the novel possible or necessary? The very terms of our question of course suggest that we ought to look to something like the Hacking thesis for an answer. And Hacking would no doubt argue that precisely those forces that open up the logical space that comes to be occupied by the mathematical theory open up the literary space that comes to be occupied by the novel. The discovery of the evidence of things makes possible the accurate calculation of chances and the science of statistics at the same time that it makes possible the concept of "ordinary life" and the self-conscious representation in language of the circumstances of that ordinary life. In one important respect, such an answer is entirely consistent with Watt's account, for it substantiates the connection Watt makes between "formal realism" and the development of new criteria for the credibility of evidence in science, philosophy, and the law. But at the same time it substantially darkens that account. It emphasizes the age's epistemological doubts, its obsessions with uncertainty, because it reminds us that if the emergence of probability marks an advance in man's intellectual progress, it is an advance that follows a fall: what we have seen Hacking subsequently call "the erosion of determinism." In order for people to imagine a technology of the uncertain, it is first necessary to grant very significant powers to *chance* and to entertain the paradoxical notion that while the accidental rules, it may itself be subject to a certain sort of system or even to a certain sort of reason. That, after all, makes possible what the medieval mind would have found inconceivable, a *science* of probability.

As ours and others' discussions of it have shown, the Hacking thesis is too good to be true. It makes the discontinuities between the concepts of probability pre- and post-1660 much more sharp than the evidence warrants. And yet as we have also seen, none of Hacking's critics has dissipated the essential interest and strength of his thesis: it remains the most intelligent account by a philosopher of what is at stake in writing about probability in the crucial period of the latter third of the seventeenth century. Far from displacing probability, chance, and uncertainty from center stage, in other words, the problems we have encountered with the thesis only strengthen our sense of their importance in the years just before modern fiction is born.

Following our own analysis of fictional probability, we should say too that the answer that gives probability its due insists on the dual standpoint of the reader and therefore on the inescapability of the realist standpoint (as well as the inescapability of an antirealist standpoint): it is precisely the kind of consciousness of the dual standpoint implicit in attributing probability to fictions that makes the novel self-conscious about problems of epistemology and about problems of point of view. The dual standpoint is what enables us to recuperate so much of Watt's account even while recognizing the problems its realist bias entails. It is of course tempting to say with Hacking (and to some degree with Watt) that there is a new concept of evidence available that makes for a new concept of probability possible. However, we know that there are concepts of internal evidence around long before the latter third of the seventeenth century—just as, by Watt's admission, the technique of formal realism was in fact available before Defoe made it the novel's primary mode.[7] Exactly what then *is* new that makes the novel possible?

I think what needs to be looked to is not so much the presence of new concepts as a growing awareness of them and willingness to use them. We know that all the knotty problems of literary probability and indeed of ordinary probability are there already in Aristotle's concept, awkwardly poised as it is between particulars and universals and between the subjective opinion of the wise and what objectively and usually happens. But of course Aristotle does not know about the antinomy of fictional probability. Nor do any Renaissance or neoclassical or even eighteenth-century writers that I am aware of. This is because they have for the most part accepted a logic of fictional probability without actually testing it or bringing it explicitly into play. Aristotle's discussions of literary probability are of course prescriptive: they tell writers to follow probability (even above possibility), but remind us that it is also probable that improbable things will happen—which notion conveniently allows much back into poetry that on the face of it is unlikely. Renaissance and neoclassical theorists similarly urge attention to probability and draw up lists of things probable and improbable. Trying to make sense of the obscurities of Aristotle's discussions, they debate the relative importance of the probable and the marvelous. But, like Aristotle, they do not bring the logic of probability into any more explicit play except than to check off elements of fictions against lists of probabilities or marvels. In effect they say: Item *A* in this poem is a *C* (for example, something attested by a Church Father). *C*s appear on my list of probabilities; so *A* is probable. One sign that the logic of probability hasn't really been tested is that definitions of the probable are either taken for granted or limited to lists; another is that theorists from Aristotle through the neoclassicals do not ask themselves *how* probable a given element of a fiction might be. In the eighteenth century however, the situation does begin substantially to change.

Douglas Patey's exposition of Augustan notions of fictional probability has revealed an elaborate theory of how probable inference was believed to work both in the process of composing fictions and of reading them. Such a theory is sufficiently subtle that for the first time it leads critics to worry about not simply whether probability is something a given fictional element either has or has not, but rather how much probability a particular element may have. Such a theory also moves well beyond a logic that consists of checking fictional items off against a list of probabilities. And accompanying this we do begin to see something genuinely novel: arguments of the sort that occur between Richardson and von Haller concerning the probability of Lovelace, for example. Before the eighteenth century, critics simply do not argue in this way. What is new here is not a particular concept of evidence, as Hacking would have it, but rather the deployment of that concept in arguments of a certain very detailed sort—arguments that

depend on very close readings and that are largely *restricted to* consideration of the evidence of things, arguments, in fact, that accept the
premises of formal realism in that they scrupulously pretend to treat
novels as veracious accounts of human experience. As we have seen,
such arguments point clearly to the antinomy of fictional probability.
Once we begin actually to weigh the evidence of a fiction against the
evidence of the real world of which it is an imitation, we make inevitable the eventual discovery of the logical oddity of ascribing probabilities to things known never to have occurred in fact.

Richardson and von Haller of course do not themselves make that
discovery. But they have made it inevitable by simultaneously taking
fictional evidence more seriously than had been done in earlier ages and
at the same time by taking the evidence of the real world more seriously. To come upon the antinomy, we need only repeat the kind of
moves they have already made until we arrive at the point that Richardson says something like, "But isn't it probable that a young man
exactly like Lovelace would behave exactly like Lovelace?" What
Richardson and von Haller can be described as doing is playing with
the fact/fiction distinction in a new way, a way that marks an important moment in the evolution of that distinction.

An ideal intellectual history of the rise of the novel would certainly
have to include a history of the distinction between fiction and fact, a
distinction that no doubt reaches its modern form through the novel
and that has been made prominent in accounts by William Nelson and
Lennard Davis.[8] And so intertwined are the relations between probability and the fact/fiction distinction that to write a history of the one is
to go some distance toward writing a history of the other. It is not a
question here of the priority, logical or generic, either of fact over
fiction or of fiction over fact, but rather of the simultaneous emergence
of each. The "novel" is no more (and no less) a derivative of "history,"
say, than "history" derives from the "novel." One cannot imagine the
one without the other, and one cannot imagine a relaxation of the
tension or competition between them, even though we may well
question the veracity of that tension by questioning the fact/fiction
distinction itself. (This is a complicated matter closely related to the

serious/nonserious distinction and about which we will have more to say presently.)

In part, the evolution of the distinction between fact and fiction depends upon changes in the concept of the true such as Hacking and Nelson have discussed. Where the medieval mind saw certainty only in the secure truths of revealed scripture, in the late Renaissance the hope becomes current that certain knowledge of history could be achieved by man on the basis of his own investigations.[9] Thus is born a modern notion of fact and of history against which fiction is to be defined. At the same time, the modern form of the fact/fiction distinction depends on its separation out of the distinction between true and false or the distinction between truth and lie. Richardson and von Haller are worried about how verisimilar *Clarissa* may be, but not, as Renaissance critics would have been, worried that it is at once verisimilar and untrue.

One thing that the modern fact/fiction distinction has freed itself from, in other words, is the liar's sense of guilt. It is notably absent from the exchange between von Haller and Richardson, which is one reason they may be described as *playing* with the fact/fiction distinction. It is a guilt that Renaissance critics, neoclassicists, and Puritans alike were aware of, albeit in varying degrees. Although there had been justifications for the lies that fictions tell from Aristotle down through the Puritans, none of the justifications quite stuck. We know that, because critics continually made and remade them. It isn't until the eighteenth century that writers and critics no longer commonly felt the need for the justification, and the concern about fictions being lies then passes almost entirely into extraliterary hands. The controversy surrounding the veracity of Defoe's *Robinson Crusoe*, often thought of as the first modern novel in English, is significant in part because it is also the *last* such controversy of any moment. The beginning of the novel is largely marked, in other words, by the end of the worry. (That the controversy amounted to as much as it did was of course due to Defoe's own always fascinating, but plainly pathological relation to lying, which has been interestingly discussed by Lennard Davis in relation to the fact/fiction distinction and the rise of the novel.[10] Although Defoe often expressed a puritanical revulsion for lies, it is hard to see signs of a sense of his own guilt for the lying that was a necessary and large part of his career as a political spy.)

Freed from a sense of guilt over the lie, writer and reader alike are free to take fiction seriously—as seriously, say, as children playing their games of pretend. They are free to pretend, in other words, that what they are playing with is real, free to repress fiction's fictionality, free to play the game that a hundred or so years later will come to be called "realism." Here we return to an important element that has run through our discussions ever since we introduced the question of pretending and that clearly deserves a prominent place in our account of the rise of the novel—the element of play. It is of course connected to the fact/fiction distinction in a variety of ways (make-believe is certainly a form of play), and any consideration of the first must inevitably return us to the other.

If to say that talk about the probability of fictions is a sign that playing is going on does not seem particularly noteworthy, that is no doubt because while make-believe and pretending are hardly fashionable topics among literary critics, and while the heyday of talk about the probability of fictions has long passed, the heyday of talk about play in art is right now. Not everything that has been written about play and art is germane to our study, but in order to see why, we need to look briefly at the history of ideas about play and especially the history of ideas about art as play.

Credit for being the first to advance a theory of art as play usually is given to Schiller, but with some significant exceptions (especially Herbert Spencer and Nietzsche), it is really only in the twentieth century that we see developed theorizing that seems, depending on one's point of view, either to exalt or reduce virtually every cultural activity to the status of play. Anthropologists, ethologists and ethnologists, economists, sociologists; theoreticians of business and of the military; psychologists, psychoanalysts, psychiatrists, and educators; historians, literary critics, philosophers, and theologians; mathematicians, computer scientists, biologists, and even physicists—virtually the entire academic community in short—have all played up play in turn.

Much of what has been written about play is however of little interest to us because it looks at play as behavior that is nonserious, a mere imitation of grown-up behavior, or worse. Herbert Spencer—good Victorian that he was—famously theorizes that the origins of play (and of art) derive from the surplus energy that higher mammals happen to have at their disposal (as their inheritance from the days in which more of a species' time was devoted to sheer survival). In this account, what has to be accounted for in play is its uselessness.[11] A certain amount of modern ethological work on play also has this character of seeking to explain behavior that apparently cannot be understood as useful, but most modern theories of play take play somewhat more seriously. Karl Groos at the turn of the century developed the now-familiar notion that in play we see preparation and practice for adult life. Thus play becomes a very serious thing indeed in every playing animal's development, but remains nonserious in that it is not the real and deadly thing that will constitute the behavior of grown-up life.[12] There is a famous and important discussion by Freud (much written about subsequently, notably by the French) of the game he calls *fort-da*, a game played by infants and analogous to peekaboo, although play is otherwise a subject on which he generally has little to say.[13] But psychoanalysis today treats play as a useful object for the study of the unconscious (along with, e.g., neurotic symptoms and dreams) and as providing a useful field on which to wage therapeutic battles on behalf of disturbed children. (The most important psychoanalytic writers on play after Freud are Erik Erikson and D. W. Winnicott.)[14] Like Groos, Jean Piaget sees in play a preparation for later life, but Piaget's interest is particularly in the role of play in the development of the child's intelligence.[15] Valuable though it may be in the development of individuals and as an object for analysis, therefore, play for such devout rationalists as both Freud and Piaget always carries with it the taint of the immature.

The most well-known, most influential, and in many respects most ambitious of twentieth-century studies is Johan Huizinga's *Homo Ludens*, which argues the grand thesis that "civilization is, in its earliest phases, played. It does not come *from* play like a babe detaching itself from the womb: it arises *in* and *as* play, and never leaves it."[16] Written

in the late thirties (and not published until 1944), the book is under-
standably grim about the prospects for play in the twentieth century. It
calls for a return to the seriousness and dignity of the play-element of
early culture, which Huizinga sees as having degenerated into mere
"puerilism, . . . that blend of adolescence and barbarity which has
been rampant all over the world for the last two or three decades."[17]
Huizinga's account is notable not only for the seriousness with which it
takes play, but for the seriousness that it sees *in* play. It is replete with
insights congenial to the argument we have made about fiction and
pretending (for example: "The child plays in complete—we can well
say, in sacred—earnest. But it plays and knows that it plays.")[18] At
the same time, Huizinga's account is only occasionally and contingently interested in play as pretending, as his definition of play—and
he notes that he is thinking specifically of the English word *play*—
makes clear: "Play is a voluntary activity or occupation executed within
certain fixed limits of time and place, according to rules freely accepted
but absolutely binding, having its aim in itself and accompanied by a
feeling of tension, joy and the consciousness it is 'different' from
'ordinary life.'"[19] What in fact is stressed here are features of games
more than of play, for this view is characterized by the centrality of
rules "absolutely binding." Described thus, play might look rather like
certain extreme forms of religious reclusion, but at the same time it is
no wonder that Huizinga sees in the institution of the law one of the
greatest manifestations of play. (Although one might object that
because in this definition play has no aim beyond itself, religious and
legal activities cannot count as play, nonetheless there is something
inconsistent in this criterion of Huizinga's definition itself. To stress the
gamelike attributes of play is precisely to imply what may not after all
be true: that in play there is always something at stake.)

Rather different in spirit and always at once more antic and more
rigorous—that is to say, more playful—is Jacques Derrida's radical
and still-evolving account of the play that is a necessary feature of
culture because it is a necessary feature of language itself. Indeed, so
pervasive and fundamental is the sense of what Derrida calls "the play
of the world" in his work that one scarcely knows where to begin in

locating his major statements about it.[20] The differential relation between signifiers out of which all meaning is generated is for Derrida an essentially playful one. So too is the relation between all those oppositions that Derrida has famously deconstructed, as between speech/writing, or serious/nonserious, or fact/fiction or literal/figurative, or identity/difference, or original/supplementary. And so too of course is the activity of deconstruction itself. Although Huizinga tells us he has in mind specifically the English word *play*, it would seem that in fact Derrida's notion more closely approaches the most general English senses of play as sheer movement and exercise. Bound by necessary limits Derrida's play certainly is, but in spirit it hardly agrees to be bound by fixed rules. In Derrida's game even the rules themselves are in play.

Pretending as such does not play a prominent role in deconstruction because (as Searle has already pointed out to us) *to pretend* is an intentional verb. And intentionality, with its implication of an idealized presence, the central human subject, is one of the concepts that deconstruction has most insistently put in question. Yet pretending as the playful movement between fact and fiction or the serious and nonserious is at the very heart of Derrida's project. It may be fair to say that, even in its most general aspects, play has for Derrida qualities that participate in pretending, for the movement of play always and necessarily involves for him ironic maskings and unmaskings.

Derrida's dispute with John Searle over the question of whether fictional discourse is "parasitic" upon ordinary discourse, as Austin had claimed, is especially apposite to our purposes, for it quite reasonably questions whether it is possible to identify the logical *priority* of fact over fiction or the serious over nonserious. It is as logical to say that we can assert things seriously because we can assert them nonseriously as that we can assert something nonseriously because we can assert things seriously. The deconstructionists' argument would be fine if it left the matter there, but of course the natural tendency is rather to reverse the hierarchy than to leave it in (playful) suspension.

His resisting this tendency is one reason Jonathan Culler's account of Derrida in *On Deconstruction* may be stronger than the original—

more faithful, that is, to Derrida than Derrida sometimes is to himself. For Culler takes great pains to emphasize again and again that the deconstruction of an opposition does not do away with that opposition, but in fact accounts for it, shows its inescapability. There is plenty of warrant for that insight in Derrida's own writings of course, but the point needs to be made because, as Culler also notices on several occasions, Derrida very much wants to reverse existing hierarchies. "I strongly and repeatedly insist,"writes Derrida, "on the necessity of the phase of reversal, which people have perhaps too swiftly attempted to discredit. . . . To neglect this phase of reversal is to forget that the structure of the opposition is one of conflict and subordination and thus to pass too swiftly, without gaining any purchase against the former opposition, to a *neutralization* which *in practice* leaves things in their former state and deprives one of any way of *intervening* effectively."[21] Adopting this logic of reversal, Derrida is thus often led to write as reductively as those he is writing against. "There has never been anything but writing, there have never been anything but substitutes and substitutional significations," he proclaims for example in *Of Grammatology*.[22] Culler may be thought of as promoting a neutralized and quietistic Derrida, but one could not entirely perversely argue that he did not go far enough, and that to pursue more ruthlessly the logic of deconstruction would lead to an even meeker position, one that explicitly celebrates precisely the oppositions it has deconstructed.

Here we have come across a considerable controversy about whether or not deconstruction is—intellectually or politically—a profoundly radical or a profoundly conservative movement.[23] And we do not entirely digress in entertaining that question, for it has I think much to do with the question of play. As we have just seen, the move that reverses a supposedly tense opposition often ends by itself becoming reductive. This is because the proponents of "facts," or the "serious," for example, want not merely to play down "fiction" and the "nonserious," but in some important way to deny them real existence, to make them in Austin's phrase "peculiarly hollow." Thus the world is reduced to "facts," everything else is denied as mere fancy, and any possible tension between fact and fiction is effectively dissipated.

Reversing such hierarchies has a similarly slackening effect, for to assert the priority or dominance of "fiction" has the effect of denying the existence of fact. The tendency of deconstructionists to reduce everything to writing and all writing in turn to the figurative and fictive has two unfortunate consequences. The first is to trivialize the meaning of figure and fiction, for insofar as *all* language is metaphorical it then can be only trivially true that any *particular* instance of language is metaphorical. The interesting and important questions then have to do with ways in which particular instances of writing may be more or less metaphorical than others; and raising those questions of course reintroduces in new form the literal/figurative distinction. The second and for our purposes more important consequence is that the reversal and reduction eliminate tension and therefore the element of play. In the terms of this study's arguments about fiction, the tendency then is to forget the dual standpoint of the reader of fictions and to pretend that we do not pretend.

It may of course be fairly objected by deconstructionists that they know all this and know it indeed far better than their critics, for it is they who have most actively theorized the inescapability of such forgetfulness—as well as the inescapability of play. And it may be objected too that in our earlier arguments about fiction we have uncritically accepted a distinction between fact and fiction, the deconstruction of which would preclude such arguments as Kendall Walton's and ours as well as Searle's. We might simply point out that it is hard to imagine a less playful sentence than one that begins, "There has never been anything but . . ."*even if* it ends with something like "play." Or if it *is* meant playfully, then that would in turn undercut deconstruction's claims to radicalism and the importance of the "phase of reversal."

In charging deconstruction with trying to have it both ways, I am falling into the trap of writing as though I had myself somehow managed to transcend the paradoxes that surround play and that make it not just difficult, but finally impossible always to keep the dual standpoint of pretending in view. But of course a major point of this study has been that to understand play is precisely to understand the inescapability of having it both ways. And from that point view we might say that the difficulty we have had in determining whether deconstruction is profoundly quietistic or profoundly radical is a sign of the power of its analysis.

Derrida's thought usefully reminds us of connections between play and the fact/fiction and serious/nonserious distinctions. We have already said something about the evolution of the former distinction; we need also briefly to consider the history of the latter, which is more plainly connected to play and which for the purposes of our study we might call the childish/grown-up distinction. We might call it that because of the explicit concern that runs throughout the history of the novel, especially in England and America, with the issue of growing up as both a theme to be treated by the novel and as a worry among critics of the novel about the nature of the novel itself. Is the novel a serious enough form for grown-ups? *Middlemarch*, Virginia Woolf tells us in a famous comment, "is one of the few English novels written for grown-up people."[24] If the novel from its beginnings has been relatively free of the guilt of the liar, it has certainly not been free from the suspicions that it is in some fundamental sense made up of the stuff of the nursery and therefore is not serious. From early in the nineteenth century on, an important justifying move has been to admit the nursery business but at the same time to insist upon *its* seriousness. This marks a line we can trace from Blake and Wordsworth on up through Dickens, Chesterton, and into twentieth-century criticism especially as it is informed by psychoanalysis. But perhaps more prominent are moves like Woolf's that assert the grown-up seriousness of at least some few novels while allowing that most are just pap. This marks a line we can trace from Austen through Thackeray and George Eliot and on to Bloomsbury.

Not accidentally, the two traditions here are broadly (and familiarly) Romantic, or antirealist, and realist respectively. For realism and the grown-up course go together. When a parent commands a child to "Be realistic!" the message is clearly to be grown-up rather than to adopt a certain narrative mode, although the ability to speak in that mode would of course be evidence that one has grown up. The assumptions that are embodied in that mode are indeed very much to the point of what it means to be grown-up. We establish that we are grown-up by attending precisely to those mundane details of ordinary life or those circumstances constituting the evidence of things that preoccupy the narrators of novels. And conversely, the technique of formal realism embodies an ideology of the grown-up: formal realism implies an ideological realism that is, above all, *serious* about life.

The category of the grown-up is of course no more eternal or central a feature of human life than is realism. It too emerges or undergoes a critical development during just the period that we have been considering as giving rise to the novel and to the modern notion of probability. Philippe Ariès' well-known *Centuries of Childhood* is often thought of as tracing the emergence of the modern idea of childhood, and so it does; but it may also be thought of as tracing the emergence of the childish/grown-up distinction, and in fact quite a lot of Ariès' study is concerned with what it means in the modern world to be an adult.[25]

Central to Ariès' view is the notion that our awareness of childhood as a qualitatively different stage of life is a relatively recent one. Before the seventeenth century, children tended to be thought of and treated as little animals or defective adults, without reason or civilization. Our modern idea of children as beings with very different but not necessarily inferior ways of thinking and capable of receiving impressions that will affect their thought and feeling throughout life developed in the seventeenth and eighteenth centuries. Thus childhood, like democracy and the individual, or like modern experimental science, or like the novel itself, becomes one of those institutions that seem indispensable today, but that turn out to have been invented out of the great religious, intellectual, and poliltical change that occurs roughly between the English Civil War and the French Revolution, between Puritanism and Romanticism.

But such an account of Ariès' thesis is itself something of a Romantic distortion, for Ariès also shows that the emergence of the modern institution of childhood involves at the same time the separation out and marking off of various kinds of behavior that were formerly common to children and grown-ups, but that have largely come to be restricted to childhood. Such activities as playing with dolls and toys, listening to fairy tales, or dressing up in elaborate costumes and disguises, were once upon a time as popular among grownups as among children, in Ariès' telling. He argues for example that toys were not originally developed to serve children, but that they evolved out of miniatures built as curios or knickknacks for grown-ups that had in turn evolved out of miniatures used as props in religious rituals, often associated with the dead.[26] Indeed, even as late as the nineteenth century, the kinds of games still today associated with children's parties were common at gatherings of grown-ups. (Recall the game of blind-man's buff at Scrooge's nephew's party in *A Christmas Carol*.) In this context, far from embodying the emergence of new behavior, the new concept of childhood represents something rather old. As Ariès puts it, "Childhood was becoming the repository of customs abandoned by the adults."[27] The new senses of *pretend* and *make-believe* associated with play that we have seen first occur towards the beginning of the nineteenth century, therefore, do not so much indicate the birth of new activities as the birth of a new consciousness, a grown-up conscious-ness, that pretends to be above childish things and that, like many a sober critic, pretends not to pretend. They mark, that is, the emergence of a new distinction.

We might summarize what we have said about the relation between realism on the one hand and probability, play, and the idea of the grown-up on the other, then, by offering the following sketch of the ethos that gives rise to the novel.

I would be inclined first of all to see in the late seventeenth and early eighteenth centuries a number of issues or problematics coming to the fore and variously connected to the legacy of Puritanism and the rise of the middle class. Central to these would be the crisis of authority that attends new doubts about the certainty of the knowledge one can hope to have about the world. Amid skeptical questions about whether one can hope to know anything with certainty, these doubts create a ten-sion between the authority of persons and the written word on the one hand and the authority of nature itself, so to speak, as manifested in the circumstances of things considered in themselves. The ability to manipulate this evidence of things is of course crucial to empiricism, the invention of modern science, and our modern category of "facts." The workings of chance, once thought to be essentially unreasonable and therefore unknowable, come to be regarded both as playing an important role in determining events and as knowable in themselves, in the aggregate or long run if not in individual cases. Thus is set up too a tension between chance and providence. (This manifests itself among other ways in a series of arguments about whether or not various statistical patterns reveal the workings of accidents or divine design.)[28] As befits a world characterized by a deep sense of uncertainty, there emerges a deep sense also of the seriousness of life and a separation out of various kinds of activity formerly common to both young and old—the development in other words of the modern childish/grown-up or nonserious/serious distinction and the modern categories of play and make-believe. And there arises as well the modern concept of fiction against the category of "fact." Although at any moment and in any writer these tensions may appear to be resolved, throughout the careers of many writers and in the period as a whole they remain conspicuous and lively. And perhaps this is why probability comes to be so important, for probability is a concept that embraces these tensions or mediates between the opposites in tension without relaxing them.

Consider for example the probable in relation to the fact/fiction distinction. Although at various points in its career probability has been more closely associated with the false or with fiction (with the opinion of the mob, for example) or more closely with fact (with universals and with the opinion of the wise, for example), the fullest accounts explicitly associate it with both equally. We noted some time ago, when considering the theories of recent philosophers, the account of Stephen Toulmin to the effect that "to say 'Probably p,' is to assert guardedly and/or with reservations, that p."[29] Such a formulation looks formally much like Walton's version of fictional assertions ("it is fictional that f," or "fictionally f," for example), and indeed both writers arrive at their respective formulations as attempts to emphasize the reality of the assertions they are interested in. Walton wants to argue (against Searle) that fictions make real assertions (although the assertions are themselves qualified in a particular way) and do not just *pretend* to make real assertions; similarly Toulmin wants to argue that probabilists make real assertions (although themselves qualified in a particular way) and do not just say what they *might* really assert had they fuller knowledge or were they more sure of themselves. He is arguing, remember, against the subjective theory of probability that says probabilistic statements are not really assertions about objective reality but assertions about one's subjective state of uncertainty. That Toulmin's argument has not diminished the energy of the subjectivists suggests that in the case of probability, as in the case of fiction, there is a *dual* standpoint necessarily to be adopted by the probabilist and no less dangerous for the philosopher to overlook than that of people who entertain fictions. But then such perhaps ought already have been our suspicion when we encountered Aristotle's probabilities poised in the gap between the universal and the particular. For while Aristotle associates the probable with the universal, the very fact that probabilities do not always occur calls them back for us into the realm of the fictional—that is, of the not-necessarily historical. To entertain a probability, no less than to entertain a fiction, is to imagine a model of how things might and perhaps ought to occur.[30] It is also necessarily to allow for the possibility that they will not occur that way at all.

What I have called the antinomy of literary probability is an outgrowth not only of the fact/fiction distinction, this is to say, but of that original ghostly quality of probability itself that puts it in two perhaps irreconcilable worlds at once and that allows us to think of it as mediating between them—much as we have seen the reader existing in and mediating between two irreconcilable worlds. Thus it is that probability also may serve as a more useful master category than realism, fact, fiction, or even the fact/fiction distinction as a whole in understanding the ethos of the rise of the novel.

Our analysis has been chiefly concerned with logical, formal, and perhaps even metaphysical questions concerning the relationship between probability and fictions. When we turn to thematic concerns the association between probability and the novel is much plainer, and there are numerous signs of the novel's intense absorption in problems of probability. Not only the fact/fiction distinction, but also the transition from the authority of books to that of things is necessarily in question when our hero is a mad knight who takes as true what he reads in romances of knight errantry. It is appropriate surely that Quixote, hero of what many have regarded as the first novel, should be a version of Buonamici's madman.[31] But more generally, the novel has from its beginnings been animated in major ways by questions of evidence and the desire for secure knowledge in the face of life's uncertainty. Consider the probabilistic echoes of such words as *fortune, adventure, hazard, providence, expectation, surprise* as well as the really vast and commonplace vocabulary having to do with probable inference or interpretation and including such words as *hope, doubt, belief, supposition, wonder,* and so on.[32] It seems fair to say that at least through the end of the nineteenth century novels are centrally concerned with people in *doubt*—and trying to get out of it.

Viewed in this way, the novel looks a lot like an instrument designed by the rising middle class to explore the varied aspects of the probable and perhaps to make manageable its reader's uneasiness with uncertainties of all sorts. The design appears especially fitting because the novel is so successful in bringing together and making relevant all the aspects of probability we have discussed. This may be too easy an explanation; for the novel, after all, voraciously brings together everything—all earlier forms of writing, all imaginable interests, and a powerful desire to somehow see it all, to work all of reality into the confines of a made-up story. It is an attractive answer nonetheless.

To give probability a leading role in the rise of the novel suggests some further projects. Douglas Patey's chapters that deal with Smollett, Fielding, Mackenzie, and Sterne have established the usefulness of looking at how novelists work with the intricacies of inference and expectation. It would obviously be interesting to extend this kind of study through the nineteenth century and try systematically to study the ways in which novels portray doubts and the logic of their resolution. It would be interesting too to look at the novel's fascination with gambling, a subject that I believe has never been undertaken in any large-scale way. While only Dostoevsky is conspicuous as a gambler among novelists, quite a bit of gambling in fact goes on in novels. Such a study of gambling might form a part of a broader study of chance in the novel. It would surely also be important to understand how it is that, from the mid-nineteenth century on, a vocabulary of the real displaces the vocabulary of the probable. It does not seem that there is any internal logic impelling this shift, for in fact talk about the probability of fictions persists to this day (as Todorov will presently remind us). But it does so in the background, as it were, while a critical vocabulary of realism and the real has been so dominant that Watt, for example, can anachronistically make realism definitive of the modern novel itself, eclipsing theories of probability almost entirely.

But most interesting for me will be to see how the study of probability may illuminate our understanding of play and the theory of fictions. I have not much hope that we can escape the double bind or antinomy of fictional probability. Nor indeed have I a real desire for such an escape. To recognize the paradoxes that haunt theories of probability, play, and fictions is however not to say that we cannot hope to develop better theories. Indeed, recognizing and accepting paradox may be just the steps necessary to arrive at new formulations. There have in fact been some suggestive developments in such diverse and unlikely areas as anthropology and mathematics that deserve a little of our attention because they suggest future directions in which our thinking about such paradoxes as are engendered by talk about fictional probability or about play may go.

Thirty years ago, Gregory Bateson advanced a theory of play inspired in part by some observations he had made of play among young monkeys. It occurred to him that at the heart of play—in this case mock combat—was the metacommunication "this is play."[33] In other words, in order for play to be possible at all, the monkeys had to exchange signals that reflexively negated their own apparent meanings. And such a metacommunication itself is logically equivalent, Bateson points out, to the paradox famously posed by Epimenides: "This statement is false." The logical equation of the statements "this is play" and "this is false" is I think warranted and possibly momentous, although I am not at all persuaded in fact that monkeys exchange signals that assert, "This is play." Perhaps they simply exchange signals that say, "Let's engage in behavior X," which has some of the features of fighting, and certainly then behavior X would closely resemble, say, behavior Y, which is real combat. Bateson has not necessarily demonstrated that monkeys understand play in the sense of understanding the *resemblance* between play and the serious, for there is not in his account a necessary *meta*communication occurring.

Be this as it may, there is no doubt that *humans* do understand the message "this is play," and from extremely early ages on. We know this because they not only actually *say*, "This is play," but because they say things like, "Pretend this is a shopping cart and you're at the store"—things that imply just the sort of dual standpoint necessary to one's entertaining fictions, in other words. And we know it also because the "metaness" of the communication becomes apparent in the fact that they not only simply play, but play with play. (I would think that for a *player* to *say*, "This is play," itself counts as playing with play.) Piaget distinguishes between the most primitive sort of play, which he calls "practice games," and a second level, which he calls "symbolic games." The first involves actions that are ends in themselves (although they will later be used seriously for survival) that do not involve thought.[34] Monkeys' mock combat could be seen as such play. The second involves make-believe and implies a conscious comparison between the real and the pretend—what we have called the dual standpoint. It is the dual standpoint that is necessary to the logical paradox of the assertion "this is play." As Bateson explains, the statement "this is play" can be unpacked to look something like this: "These actions in which we now engage do not denote what those actions *for which they stand* would denote."[35] The paradox enters because the words "for which they stand" are themselves equivalent to "denote," giving the following expanded version of "this is play": "These actions, in which we now engage, do not denote what would be denoted by those actions which these actions denote."[36] This is of course illogical, a classic case of having it both ways. (Not coincidentally, perhaps, it was Bateson who coined the term "double bind.")

What makes Bateson's identification of self-conscious pretending with Epimenides' paradox seem possibly momentous to me is the use to which the paradox has been put by Douglas Hofstadter in his elaborate exposition of Gödel's theorem in *Gödel, Escher, Bach: An Eternal Golden Braid.*[37] Gödel's theorem is one of those great twentieth-century inventions like relativity and the unconscious that have radically undermined scientistic and positivistic faiths in our hopes of achieving some ultimate certainty or understanding of things. Most simply, the theorem says that all consistent axiomatic formulations of number theory (or of similar axiomatic systems) will contain statements that are true but unprovable within the system. Such statements are themselves therefore undecidable, and their existence means that such axiomatic systems are themselves logically incomplete. What makes Gödel's theorem possible is the power of axiomatic systems like number theory to generate propositions logically equivalent to Epimenides' paradox— propositions that assert not that "this is false," but that "this proposition has no proof." The propositions are true because generated according to the rules of the system, but unprovable because the system is not powerful enough to generate a proof for them. As in Epimenides' formulation, the paradox is generated by the power of statements to refer to themselves, to be metastatements, in other words, or, as Hofstadter likes to put it, the power to jump out of the system.

Hofstadter's work is in artificial intelligence, and his deepest interests are in the nature of mind itself, whether artificial or natural. He shares with Derrida a fascination for discovering and tinkering with paradoxes, but whereas Derrida is forever the skeptic, ironizing and problematizing, Hofstadter clearly likes the role of the whiz kid who can figure the puzzle out—that is, solve it. Recognizing very much the sort of problems Derrida poses, problems that subvert our sense of such notions as reference and communication as transparent, Hofstadter wants to know how it is that our minds work as well as they do and allow us to get on at all. Like Derrida also, and like Richard Rorty (or like Gödel himself, for that matter), working within a particular system he has arrived at some positions that seem entirely opposed to his original orientation and that look a lot like those of rival systems. Computer scientists are expected to be people who believe we are nothing but machines. Hofstadter does in fact believe that minds are constituted by running programs of a certain sort, with no additional metaphysical entities complicating the works; but he is no reductionist. He is not one to say, that is, that we are *nothing but* programs running, for he fully understands the likelihood that the mind-body problem is a problem of multiple point of view.

His chief intuition, of course a long way from being susceptible to experiment, is that self-referential loops like those in Epimenides' paradox or Gödel's theorem will prove to be the keys to our understanding of mind. If he is right, that will in turn mean that the logical equivalents of pretending or probabilistic thinking or of figurative language are the very essence of mind and that really to understand mind—for people in artificial intelligence the final aim is to run programs that cannot practically be distinguished from the operations of a mind—will presuppose the understanding of pretending or thinking metaphorically or probabilistically. The grand and ultimate hope here is for a technology of mind, of metaphor, and of pretending. Such a technology, for all its Frankensteinian potential, would not do away with figure or fiction or the inductive leap from fact to forecast, but would be instead their ultimate vindication.

OUR SECOND large practical question concerns the consequences of our analysis for criticism. If we grant the validity of the arguments we have made about the antinomy of fictional probability and its relation to the problem of literary belief; if we agree that talk about literary probability is not only the sign that pretending is going on, but the sign of a peculiarly dynamic and self-conscious sort of pretending that embraces the dual standpoint of the reader; then we still need to ask how this conclusion may be expected to affect criticism. Insofar as the argument has tried to describe some general things that go on whenever we read fictions, I do not think we need to look for consequences among the ways in which we read particular fictions. My argument does not urge us to make any changes in the way we actually read, nor does it really imagine changes as immediately possible. That is why this study offers no readings of particular fictions. Insofar as it has discussed the significance of the ways in which we discuss fictions, however, there does seem to me an important if awkward consequence. The antinomy of fictional probability and its necessary involvement in pretending make consideration of the probability of fictions at once inadmissible and unavoidable: it puts the critic in a classic double bind.

The inadmissibility of talk of literary probability is of course nowadays widely recognized. Writing an introduction to a series of essays in an issue of the French journal *Communication* devoted to the *vraisemblable*, Tzvetan Todorov tells us: "The concept of the *vraisemblable* is no longer in fashion. It isn't found in "serious" scientific writing; on the other hand, it is still all the rage in commentaries of the second rank, in scholarly editions of classics, and in the classroom." Todorov then quotes several extracts from a commentary on *Le Mariage du Figaro* that appeal to criteria of the *vraisemblable* and adds:

> The term *vraisemblable* is here used in its most naïve sense of "conforming to reality." One calls certain actions and attitudes improbable because they do not seem capable of being produced in reality. Corax, the first theoritician of the *vraisemblable*, had already gone much farther: the *vraisemblable* was not for him a relation with the real (as is the *vrai*), but with what the majority believe to be the real—in other words, with public opinion.[38]

Perhaps the most important conclusion of my argument would be that it is impossible to choose between the naïveté of critics like the commentator on Beaumarchais, who confidently appeals to standards of probability in fictions, or the naïveté of Todorov, who confidently appeals to a sophisticated "scientific" standard that pretends it has transcended pretending. Todorov is no doubt more clever than the commentator on Beaumarchais; in his (of course false) claim that Corax of Syracuse knew more than the modern scholar by understanding that probability is a matter of opinion and therefore of convention,

Todorov thereby adroitly appears to rescue for modern delectation (the conventional now being in fashion once again) virtually all discussion of literary probability through the eighteenth century. Corax's definition is of course the one handed down to and accepted by Plato (what the mob believe) rather than the one accepted by Aristotle (what the wise believe). But the aspect of probability that is in some form associated with opinion remains in view until quite recently; indeed, one could say that its modern heir is the subjective theory of probability. In dismissing those aspects of literary probability that assume some actual (even if highly problematic) relation between literature and the real or true, however, Todorov ignores everything that has made the question of the probable interesting to literary theory since Aristotle, who was the first to make such a relation to the real a part of the definition.

More positively, we could say that our conclusion is that the commentator on Beaumarchais and Todorov equally deserve our understanding and attention, for the double bind of fictional probability still traps the literary antiprobabilist no less than the literary probabilist. Todorov can appear superior to the naïve probabilist by inhabiting a system that is outside that of the commentator on Beaumarchais and appears therefore to have the more inclusive view. We have seen however that this standpoint, with its apparently wider perspective, is itself partially a matter of pretend—particularly in that it pretends itself not to adopt the narrower standpoint of one who entertains a fiction. But in stepping back from Todorov's position and standing as it were above it, we must be careful not to give the appearance of ourselves occupying a loftier ground—at least not one that carries us beyond the trap of the double bind. While it is certainly desirable in general to be as explicit as possible about the frame of reference from which we are operating at any moment when a fiction is in question, the trap catches us no matter how self-conscious and distant we try to be. For the essence of entertaining fictions is to inhabit a dual standpoint while denying that there is more than one frame at all. That, after all, is what allows fictional beliefs to consort with real beliefs and in the process change them and change the world.

Notes

Introduction

1. A good and not very technical account of the modern sciences that rely upon a probabilistic definition of information is Jeremy Campbell, *Grammatical Man* (New York: Simon and Schuster, 1982). See Jacques Monod, *Chance and Necessity: An Essay on the Natural Philosophy of Modern Biology,* trans. Austryn Wainhouse (New York: Alfred A. Knopf, 1971) for a recent discussion of the controversy among biologists concerning the role of chance in natural selection.

2. Ian Hacking, *The Emergence of Probability* (Cambridge: Cambridge University Press, 1975) and *The Logic of Statistical Inference* (Cambridge: Cambridge University Press, 1965); Michel Foucault, *The Order of Things* (New York: Pantheon, 1977).

3. Ian Hacking, "The Erosion of Determinism," in Jaakko Hintikka, David Gruedner, and Evandro Agazzi, eds., *Probabilistic Thinking, Thermodynamics, and the Interaction of the History and Philosophy of Science* (Dordrecht: D. Reidel, 1981), p. 107.

4. Ibid., p. 120.

5. Barbara Shapiro, *Probability and Certainty in Seventeenth-Century England* (Princeton: Princeton University Press, 1983).

6. Paula Backscheider, *Probability, Time, and Space in Eighteenth-Century Literature* (New York: AMS Press, 1979).

7. Douglas Lane Patey, *Probability and Literary Form: Philosophic Theory and Literary Practice in the Auguston Age* (Cambridge: Cambridge University Press, 1984).

8. Jerome Bruner, *Actual Minds, Possible Worlds* (Cambridge, Mass.: Harvard University Press, 1986) is an excellent account by a distinguished cognitive scientist of many of the ways in which theories of fiction are emerging as important to the study of mind itself.

9. An obvious exception would be explicit literary critical discussions in novels which self-consciously call attention to a novel's fictionality, as in the introductory chapters to the books of *Tom Jones*. It could of course be objected from various quarters that even statements made by historians about Waterloo and by physicists about electrons are in some deep sense fictional, nor would I deny the power of the arguments that lie behind such objections. Nevertheless, this study does assume that there is an essential difference between the kind of fiction I entertain when I talk about Mr. Pickwick—whom nobody takes as ever having been a real person—and the kind I entertain when I talk about Napoleon or electrons.

Chapter I
Aristotle

1. For example, J. H. Freese in his translation of the *'Art' of Rhetoric* in the Loeb Classical Library edition of Aristotle's works (1926; reprint, Cambridge, Mass.: Harvard University Press, 1975), p. 10 n. *a*. I shall quote Freese's translation except where noted.

2. I quote the translation in Edith Hamilton and Huntington Cairns, eds., *The Complete Dialogues of Plato* (1963; reprint, Princeton: Princeton University Press, Bollingen Series, 1980).

3. I quote A. J. Jenkinson's translation in vol. 1 of W. D. Ross, ed., *The Works of Aristotle* (1928; reprint, Oxford: Oxford University Press, 1963).

4. The translation is by R. C. Jebb and the edition by J. E. Sandys (Cambridge: Cambridge University Press, 1909).

5. W. D. Ross, *Aristotle's Prior and Posterior Analytics: A Revised Text with Introduction and Commentary* (1949; reprint, Oxford: Clarendon, 1965), p. 500.

6. I use the translation by Gerald F. Else in his *Aristotle's Poetics: The Argument* (Cambridge, Mass.: Harvard University Press, 1967).

7. Ibid., p. 305.

8. In *Aristotle's Poetics* Else, for no reason I am aware of, here translates *to eikos* as "plausibility."

9. Else, *Aristotle's Poetics,* p. 551.

10. Again I adapt Else's translation; his reads: "One should . . . choose impossibilities that are (made) plausible in preference to possibilities that are (left) implausible."

11. Else omits all discussion of chap. 25. This translation is an amalgam of S. H. Butcher's, Ingram Bywater's, Leon Golden's, G. M. A. Grube's, and Kenneth A. Telford's together with my own rude attempts to grapple with the original.

12. It might seem plausible to object further that in any case Aristotle is contradicting himself relative to the discussion of probable impossibles, because if it is now a question how to justify an improbability or illogicality, then it would follow that the injunction to value probability before possibility has already been violated. But *is* that the question? At the beginning of the passage, the question posed had to do with justifying impossibles; the confusion here arises from the fact that Aristotle has let his topic slip from justifying what cannot in actuality occur to justifying the merely unreasonable *(alogos)*.

13. In *Fact, Fiction, and Forecast,* 3d ed. (New York: Bobbs-Merrill, 1973), Nelson Goodman writes that he has "solved or dissolved" the problem (p. 59). His important contribution to the philosophy of science does not, however, solve the problem in the sense of providing an answer that in my terms fills in any of the gaps; rather it says that the problem as posed is unanswerable and that if we want to make progress in thinking about induction we need to find out how people actually *do* arrive at inductions and write some good rules that reflect that process.

Chapter II
Hacking's Novelty

1. Bernard Weinberg, *A History of Literary Criticism in the Italian Renaissance,* 2 vols. (Chicago: Chicago University Press, 1961), 1:349.

2. Edmund F. Byrne, *Probability and Opinion: A Study in the Medieval Presuppositions of Post-Medieval Theories of Probability* (The Hague: Martinus Nijhoff, 1968), p. 188. And see Hacking, *Emergence of Probability,* p. 23.

3. Hacking, *Emergence of Probability,* pp. 23–25.

4. Ibid., p. 16.

5. See Richard Rorty, *Philosophy and the Mirror of Nature* (Princeton: Princeton University Press, 1979), esp. chap. 7 and "Method, Social Science, and Social Hope," *Canadian Journal of Philosophy* 11 (1981): 569–601; see also Ian Hacking, "Michel Foucault's Immature Science," *Noûs* 13 (1979): 39–51.

6. Hacking, *Emergence of Probability*, pp. 8–9.

7. Ibid., p. 9.

8. Ibid., p. 39.

9. Ibid., p. 42.

10. Ibid., p. 32.

11. Ibid., p. 34.

12. Ibid.

13. Antoine Arnauld, *The Art of Thinking: Port-Royal Logic*, trans. James Dickoff and Patricia James (New York: Bobbs-Merrill, 1964), pp. 342–343. And see Hacking, *Emergence of Probability*, p. 79.

14. Richard von Mises, *Probability, Statistics, and Truth*, 2d ed. (1957; reprint, New York: Dover, 1981), p. 4, and see also p. vi.

15. Ian Hacking, *Why Does Language Matter to Philosophy?* (Cambridge: Cambridge University Press, 1975).

16. Hacking, *Emergence of Probability*, p. 54.

17. Ibid., p. 56.

18. S. Sambursky, "On the Possible and the Probable in Ancient Greece," *Osiris* 12 (1956): 35–48 and O. B. Sheynin, "On the Prehistory of the Theory of Probability," *Archive for History of Exact Sciences* 12 (1974): 97–141. And see also Edward H. Madden, "Aristotle's Treatment of Probability and Signs," *Philosophy of Science* 24 (1957): 167–172.

19. Ivo Schneider's paper is in Jaakko Hintikka, David Gruedner, and Evandro Agazzi, eds., *Probabilistic Thinking, Thermodynamics, and the Interaction of the History and Philosophy of Science* (Dordrecht: D. Reidel, 1981), pp. 3–24; Daniel Garber and Sandy Zabell's is in *Archive for History of Exact Sciences* 21 (1979): 33–53; Patey's contribution is appendix A of *Probability and Literary Form*, pp. 266–273.

20. Hacking, "Erosion of Determinism," pp. 105–123.

21. Ibid., p. 121.

22. Patey, *Probability and Literary Form*, p. 273; Garber and Zabell, "On the Emergence," p. 49; and Schneider, "Why Do We Find?" pp. 5–6.

23. Sambursky, "On the Possible," pp. 38–39, 46–47.

24. Hacking, *Emergence of Probability*, pp. 6–8, 17.

25. See Hume's own summary in "An Abstract of a Treatise of Human Nature," in Antony Flew, ed., *On Human Nature and the Understanding* (New York: Collier, 1962, pp. 286–302) and book 1, part 3, section 6 of the *Treatise* itself.

Chapter III
Ambiguity and the Modern Concept of Probability

1. Hacking, *Emergence of Probability,* pp. 11–17.

2. Ibid., p. 12.

3. Ibid.

4. Rudolf Carnap, *The Logical Foundations of Probability* (Chicago: University of Chicago Press, 1950).

5. Max Black, "Probability," in Paul Edwards, ed., *The Encyclopedia of Philosophy* (New York: Macmillan and the Free Press, 1972), 6: 468.

6. Hacking, *Emergence of Probability,* p. 15.

7. Ibid., pp. 12–13.

8. And see also the views of William Kneale, *Probability and Induction* (Oxford: Clarendon, 1949), pp. 9–13.

9. Black, "Probability," p. 477.

10. Stephen E. Toulmin, *The Uses of Argument* (Cambridge: Cambridge University Press, 1958), pp. 62 and 65.

11. J. N. Findlay, "Probability without Nonsense," *The Philosophical Quarterly* 2 (1952): 219.

12. Toulmin, *Uses of Argument,* p. 85.

13. Kneale, *Probability and Induction,* p. 20.

14. Toulmin, *Uses of Argument,* pp. 62–66.

15. Hacking, *Emergence of Probability,* p. 15.

Chapter IV
In the Renaissance

1. Baxter Hathaway, *Marvels and Commonplaces: Renaissance Literary Criticism* (New York: Random House, 1968), p. vii. I am heavily indebted to Hathaway in what follows.

2. Ibid., pp. 76–77.

3. Weinberg, *History of Literary Criticism,* 1: 630.

4. Hathaway, *Marvels,* p. 61. Is there also a mistake here? Does Castelvetro not perhaps more likely mean that animals *with* reason are marvels?

5. Ibid., p. 66.

6. See Robert M. Grant, *Miracle and Natural Law in Graeco-Roman and Early Christian Thought* (Amsterdam: North-Holland Publishing, 1952) for a thorough survey of the early history of thought about the miraculous. For a recent collection of modern discussions, see C. F. D. Moule, ed., *Miracles: Cambridge Studies in Their Philosophy and History* (London: A. R. Mowbray, 1965).

7. Quoted by Hathaway, *Marvels*, pp. 78–79.

8. Quoted by Weinberg, *History of Literary Criticism*, 2: 695.

9. Hathaway, *Marvels*, pp. 83–84.

10. We will also more generally be haunted by the "mad and imbecile." As I have—I believe—no knowledge about the experience of "imbeciles" at plays, I should note that the term is used here of course in no technical sense, but merely as a borrowing from Buonamici to recall his discussion of signs and to remind us that there is plainly something wrong with anyone who wholly mistakes the fictional representations in a play or novel or any work of art for "real" things and events.

11. Quoted by Hathaway, *Marvels* p. 84.

12. Quoted by Weinberg, *History of Literary Criticism*, 2: 697.

13. Weinberg, in *History of Literary Criticism*, reads the definition somewhat differently than I and sees nature playing a greater role in the establishment of verisimilitude. (Opinion, it also should be said, is for Buonamici a function of the imagination, which does not follow the logic of necessity alone, but that of probability.)

14. Hathaway, *Marvels*, pp. 80–81.

15. Weinberg, *History of Literary Criticism*, 1: 392.

16. Quoted by Hathaway, *Marvels*, p. 81.

17. Weinberg, *History of Literary Criticism*, 2: 697.

18. Recall that Plato tells us the probable *(to eikos)* is "like truth" and that *verisimilis* is the Latin rendering of the Greek.

19. J. E. Spingarn, *A History of Literary Criticism in the Renaissance*, 2d ed. (New York: Columbia University Press, 1908), pp. 3–4 passim.

20. William Nelson, *Fact or Fiction: The Dilemma of the Renaissance Storyteller* (Cambridge, Mass.: Harvard University Press, 1973).

21. See, for example, Raymond Macdonald Alden, "The Doctrine of Verisimilitude in French and English Criticism of the Seventeenth Century," in, *Matzke Memorial Volume* (Stanford, Calif.: Stanford University, 1911), pp. 38–48.

Chapter V
In the Age of the Rise of the Novel

1. See "Introduction," n. 7 and chap. 2, n. 19.

2. Patey, *Probability and Literary Form*, pp. 88–89.

3. Ibid., p. 26.

4. Quoted by Patey, *Probability and Form*, p. 33.

5. Quoted by Alden, "Doctrine of Verisimilitude," pp. 45–46.

6. In addition to Patey, see Hoyt Trowbridge, *From Dryden to Jane Austen: Essays on English Critics and Writers, 1660–1818* (Albuquerque: University of New Mexico Press, 1977), esp. the chap. "White of Selbourne: The Ethos of Probabilism," and Wallace Jackson, *The Probable and the Marvelous: Blake, Wordsworth, and the Eighteenth-Century Critical Tradition* (Athens, Ga.: University of Georgia Press, 1978).

7. That is a sense that the ancestors of *probability* had had at least since Plato used *to eikos* to refer to what the ignorant believe. But interestingly *probability* has never had such a pejorative sense in English, and no single word had such a sense either until *verisimilitude* acquired it late in the 1700s. A pejorative sense of *probability*, in other words, had in English to be newly coined.

8. Jackson, *The Probable and Marvelous*, p. 11.

9. For the purposes of surveying the widest possible range of eighteenth-century literary criticism and theory on the novel, I have found no better aid than Ioan Williams, ed., *Novel and Romance, 1700–1800: A Documentary Record* (New York: Barnes and Noble, 1970). Williams samples discussions in prefaces, reviews, essays, and correspondence, and the majority of his selections are otherwise difficult to obtain, often coming from very scarce sources. (He omits all of Fielding's writings on the novel on the basis of their accessibility.) Chesterfield's allusion to "the bounds of probability" is in Williams, p. 101; Johnson's is in *Rambler*, No. 4.

10. Quoted by H. T. Swedenberg, Jr., *The Theory of the Epic in England: 1650–1800*, University of California Publications in English, vol. 15 (Berkeley and Los Angeles: University of California Press, 1944), p. 22. My translation.

11. These examples all appear in Williams, *Novel and Romance*, pp. 156, 162, 250, 366, 393, 409.

12. Paul K. Alkon, "The Odds against Friday: Defoe, Bayes, and Inverse Probability," in Paula R. Backscheider, ed., *Probability, Time, and Space in Eighteenth-Century Literature* (New York: AMS Press, 1979), pp. 29–61.

13. From *An Essay on the New Species of Writing Founded by Mr. Fielding: With a Word or Two upon the Modern State of Criticism* (London: William Owen, 1751), quoted in Williams, *Novel and Romance*, p. 154.

14. Hacking, *Emergence of Probability*, p. 122. Equal possibilities are a necessary part of the classical definition of mathematical probability as the ratio of favorable cases to total number of equipossible ones. Thus the probability of an arbitrary favorable case—throwing a two, say, with a die—is ⅙: 1 is the number of favorable cases (there is only one way to throw a two with a single die) and 6 is the number of equipossible cases (the number of sides of the die, each of which is assumed to be equally likely to be thrown). Probabilities are mathematically expressed as ratios or in decimal notation as numbers between 0 and 1: 0 and 1 both express certainties (the certainty of no probability or of absolute probability); .5 expresses equipossibility.

15. John Arbothnot, "An Argument for Divine Providence Taken from the Constant Regularity Observed in the Births of Both Sexes," *Philosophical Transactions of the Royal Society of London* 27 (1710): 186–190.

16. Quoted by Williams, *Novel and Romance*, pp. 139–140.

17. Of course one should recognize that "the way things actually are" cannot be perceived except through what is in itself in a sense an utterance, or at least has the form of an utterance: for one perceives things of course not directly but as already highly organized and articulated—even theorized—structures. But I mean to point simply to the more obvious differences between looking at books and looking at other kinds of things.

18. Ian Watt, *The Rise of the Novel* (Berkeley: University of California Press, 1959). See also Patey's extensive discussion of "circumstances" in *Probability and Literary Form*, esp. pp. 50–62.

19. Watt, *Rise of the Novel*, p. 32.

20. In *Dickens on the Romantic Side of Familiar Things* (New York: Columbia University Press, 1977), pp. 129–135, I have discussed some of these inconsistencies.

21. Some recent books that offer powerful and sophisticated arguments sympathetic to realism despite full awareness of the theoretical problems with it are John Romano, *Dickens and Reality* (New York: Columbia University Press, 1977); Jonathan Arac, *Commissioned Spirits: The Shaping of Social Motion in Dickens, Carlyle, Melville, and Hawthorne* (New Brunswick: Rutgers University Press, 1979); Robert L. Caserio, *Plot, Story, and the Novel* (Princeton: Princeton University Press, 1979); and Elizabeth Deeds Ermarth, *Realism and Consensus in the English Novel* (Princeton: Princeton University Press, 1983).

Chapter VI
The Antinomy of Literary Probability

1. See Patey's discussion of this distinction in *Probability and Literary Form,* pp. 142–145 and 163.

2. Note that this is not the same as calculating a precise probability for my uncle as an individual, which most mathematicians would regard as absurd. See, for example, von Mises, *Probability,* pp. 17–18.

3. David Lewis, "Truth in Fiction," *American Philosophical Quarterly* 15 (1978): 37–46.

4. Notice also that the "reasonable" probability statements we have come up with stand up in part because the examples chosen are extreme. No one has trouble in assenting to the proposition that Lovelace is a more probable character than Superman. But if we take a question more likely to come up in actual criticism, such as, How probable a character is Lovelace vis-à-vis Clarissa? then the meaning of the question becomes much murkier.

5. The possibility of the narrator's unreliability of course adds a complication and makes for a special case. But even in this special case we must base an attribution of unreliability upon the evidence of the text, and *this* we must accept as certain and fixed in a way that no evidence drawn from the real world can ever be. So the unreliability of narrators plays itself out within peculiarly definite constraints.

6. Unless we use an eighteenth-century idiom in which the vocabulary of reality and nature are drawn into what is logically a probabilistic discussion. See the following discussion of Fanny Burney's appeal to nature.

7. An antinomy is properly speaking a contradiction between propositions that seem equally reasonable, not simply a logical oddity or absurdity. But I want to use the term *antinomy* here to anticipate what our analysis of pretending will lead us to conclude about the oddity: that it is the very nature of our ability to entertain fictions that leads us on the one hand to want to ascribe probability to them while on the other we must recognize the illegitimacy of such ascriptions.

8. From *The Analytic Review,* May 1793, quoted by Williams, *Novel and Romance,* p 378.

9. From his *Dissertations Moral and Critical,* quoted by Williams, *Novel and Romance,* p. 309.

10. This is in fact an assumption Clara Reeve makes in her famous distinction in *The Progress of Romance* between novel and romance (in Miriam Allott,

ed., *Novelists on the Novel* [London: Routledge and Kegan Paul, 1965], p. 47): "The Novel is a picture of real life and manners, and of the times in which it was written. The Romance in lofty and elevated language describes what never happened nor is likely to happen.—The Novel gives a familiar relation of such things, as pass every day before our eyes, such as may happen to a friend, or to ourselves; and the perfection of it, is to represent every scene, in so easy and natural a manner, and to make them appear so probable, as to deceive us into a persuasion (at least while we are reading) that all is real until we are affected by the joys or distresses, of the persons in the story, as if they were our own."

11. For the opposite view, see Kneale, *Probability and Induction,* pp. 9–10. His view is the occasion for Toulmin's discussion quoted in this paragraph.

12. Black, "Probability," p. 465.

13. Toulmin, *Uses of Argument,* p. 54.

14. Hacking, *Emergence of Probability,* p. 19. See also Patey's discussion of this, *Probability and Literary Form,* pp. 270–271.

Chapter VII
Fictional Belief

1. J. L. Austin, *How to Do Things with Words,* ed. J. O. Urmson (Cambridge, Mass.: Harvard University Press, 1962), p. 101.

2. Austin, *How to Do Things,* p. 22. And see the discussion of this point by Wolfgang Iser, *The Act of Reading: A Theory of Aesthetic Response* (Baltimore: Johns Hopkins University Press, 1978), pp. 58–61.

3. John Searle, "The Logical Status of Fictional Discourse," *New Literary History* 6 (1975): 319–332.

4. In Jacques Derrida, *Margins of Philosophy,* trans. Alan Bass (Chicago: University of Chicago Press, 1982), pp. 307–330 and *Glyph* 2 (1977): 162–254 respectively.

5. "The answer seems to me obvious, though not easy to state precisely," Searle says in "Logical States," p. 324. Is it significant that he chose chiefly literary people as his audience in this essay?

6. Ibid., p. 325.

7. Ibid.

8. Ibid., p. 326. It isn't clear if Searle knows he's echoing Austin's term.

9. In addition to the essays cited above, see Jonathan Culler's exposition of Derrida's analysis in his *On Deconstruction* (Ithaca: Cornell University Press, 1982), esp. pp. 110–121.

10. Of course this question of the relevance of authorial intention continues to be controversial. An extremely interesting contribution that manages also to survey the important positions from the New Critics forward and that centers on Stephen Knapp and Walter Benn Michael's argument that intention and meaning are in fact the same thing can be found in W. J. T. Mitchell, ed., *Against Theory: Literary Studies and the New Pragmatism* (Chicago: University of Chicago Press, 1985).

11. Searle, "Logical Status," p. 321.

12. Ibid., p. 325.

13. At least one dictionary, *Webster's New International,* 2d ed., puts Searle's deceptive and nondeceptive senses together under one numbered sense: "To hold out the appearance of being, possessing, or performing; to profess, to make believe; to make pretense; to feign; sham; as, to *pretend* to be asleep."

14. Kendall Walton, "Pictures and Make-Believe," *The Philosophical Review* 82 (1973): 283–319; "Are Representations Symbols?" *The Monist* 58 (1974): 236–254; "Points of View in Narrative and Depictive Representation," *Noûs* 10 (1976): 49–63; "Fearing Fictions," *The Journal of Philosophy* 75 (1978): 5–27; "How Remote Are Fictional Worlds from the Real World?" *The Journal of Aesthetics and Art Criticism* 37 (1978): 11–23; "Fiction, Fiction-Making, and Styles of Fictionality," *Philosophy and Literature* 7 (1983): 78–88.

15. Walton, "Fiction, Fiction-Making," pp. 85–86. Compare Knapp and Michael's account of the waves that produce "A slumber did my spirit seal" in Mitchell, *Against Theory,* pp. 15–17.

16. Walton, "Fiction, Fiction-Making," p. 84.

17. It is especially in "Pictures and Make-Believe" that Walton works out these forms, but he makes use of them in all the articles previously cited in n. 14.

18. Walton, "Fiction, Fiction-Making," p. 87.

19. Ibid. It is because Walton's argument implies that we need not consider fictions as the product of anyone's actions that his theory is radically different from those that have traditionally occupied both literary theory and philosophy, especially the tradition of Nelson Goodman that most recently has been enriched by the important work of Nicholas Wolterstorff in *Works and Worlds of Art* (Oxford: Clarendon, 1980). Wolterstorff discusses Walton's theory on pp. 317–325.

20. Walton, "Fearing Fictions," p. 7.

21. Ibid., pp. 8–9. Of course a psychoanalyst might well speak of (unconscious) beliefs as behind such automatic, involuntary reactions.

22. Ibid., p. 9.

23. Ibid., p. 14.

24. Jorge Luis Borges "Everything and Nothing," in *Labyrinths: Selected Stories and Other Writings,* ed. Donald A. Yates and James E. Irby (New York: New Directions, 1962), p. 218 and quoted in Walton, "Fearing Fictions," p. 12.

25. Walton, "Fearing Fictions," p. 19.

26. Walton, "How Remote?" p. 11. Perhaps the best comic example of such interactions between real and fictional worlds occurs in Woody Allen's story "The Kugelmass Episode" in *Side Effects* (New York: Ballantine Books, 1981). Kugelmass, a professor of literature, fulfills his dream of entering *Madame Bovary* with the help of a magician. While he's dallying with Emma, students across the country are asking their teachers, "Who is this character on page 100? A bald Jew is kissing Madame Bovary?" And after Kugelmass succeeds in getting himself and Emma *out* of the book, a professor at Stanford wonders: "First a strange character named Kugelmass, and now she's gone from the book. Well, I guess the mark of a classic is that you can reread it a thousand times and always find something new."

27. Walton, "How Remote?" p. 12.

28. Ibid., p. 13.

29. Ibid.

30. Ibid., pp. 14–15.

31. Ibid., p. 15.

32. Ibid.

33. Ibid., p. 17.

34. Ibid., p. 18.

35. See esp. Walton, "How Remote?" p. 14.

36. Walton, "Fearing Fictions", p. 25.

37. Walton, "How Remote?" p. 19.

38. Ibid., p. 20 and "Fearing Fictions," pp. 20–21.

39. Walton, "Fearing Fictions," p. 20.

40. Walton, "How Remote?" p. 20.

41. Others have tried to rescue the reality of our psychological attitudes toward fictional entities in no less strictly logical accounts. See Harold Skulsky, "On Being Moved by Fiction," *The Journal of Aesthetics and Art Criticism* 39 (1980): 5–14. I don't agree with Skulsky's argument, though I too want to consider our attitudes toward fictional entities "real" attitudes.

42. Walton, "How Remote?" p. 21.

43. Samuel Taylor Coleridge, *Shakespearean Criticism,* ed. Thomas Middleton Raysor, 2 vols. (London: J. M. Dent and Sons, 1960), 1: 115–116; see also 1: 179.

44. In chap. 14 of *Biographia Literaria.*

45. It is also interesting that, although his subject is *dramatic* illusion, Coleridge turns to a reader of *novels* for his example of the psychology of the audience.

46. Walton, "Fearing Fictions," p. 7.

47. Ibid., p. 14n.

48. Ibid., p. 13.

49. Skulsky, "On Being Moved."

50. Skulsky for example takes it as evidence that there is no make-believe in one's looking at a painting and saying something like, "Look at those satyrs galloping away from us near the middle of the canvas" ("On Being Moved," p. 6). Such "mixed idioms," however, point precisely to the dual standpoint of the make-believer, who simultaneously talks about fictional objects as real ("satyrs galloping") and as fictional ("in the middle of the canvas").

51. Walton, "Fearing Fictions," p. 10.

52. In "How Can We Fear and Pity Fictions?" *The British Journal of Aesthetics* 21 (1981): 291-304, Peter Lamarque offers the counterargument that in responding to fictions we have real emotions toward "mental representations or thought-contents . . . quite independently of beliefs we might hold about being in personal danger or about the existence of real suffering or pain" (p. 296). This seems to me to beg the question of pretending.

53. Indeed, in the *Sophist* (esp. 240b–c), it is just this contradictoriness of fictions (images), their being at once real and not real, that particularly exercises Plato, and in the *Republic,* book 10, the law of the excluded middle is specifically brought in (602e) to point out how far art is removed from the truth (603b–c).

54. Roland Barthes, *The Pleasure of the Text,* trans. Richard Miller (New York: Hill and Wang, 1973), pp. 3–4.

55. See esp. chap. 2, the third section, "Stories of Reading," in Culler's *On Deconstruction,* pp. 64–84. See also Marian Hobson's very interesting book *The Object of Art: The Theory of Illusion in Eighteenth-Century France* (Cambridge: Cambridge University Press, 1982) for its account of the experience of illusion as "bimodal," pp. 47–50, as well as the connections it draws between probability *(vraisemblance)* and illusion, pp. 32–38.

56. Culler, *On Deconstruction,* p. 67.

57. Jonathan Culler, "Problems in the Theory of Fiction," *Diacritics* 14 (1984): 3.

58. Thomas Nagel, "Brain Bisection and the Unity of Consciousness," in John Perry, ed., *Personal Identity* (Berkeley: University of California Press, 1975), p. 232. Nagel presents a good summary of work done with split-brain patients and good bibliographic information.

59. Ibid., pp. 241–242.

60. Ibid., pp. 242–243.

61. John D. Patterson, "The Neurophysiology of Binocular Vision," *Scientific American*, August 1972, p. 84.

Chapter VIII
Fictional Probability

1. Joseph Conrad, "Heart of Darkness," in *Youth: And Two Other Stories* (New York: McClure, Phillips and Co., 1903), p. 152.

2. Certainly among such general beliefs would be the kinds of propositions that Aristotle considers to be probabilities, such as that "the envious hate." The similarity once again points out the close connections between belief and probability. But there is too an important difference. Because they have a foot in the realm of universals, Aristotle's probabilities provide an unchanging standard against which poetry is judged, whereas the sort of beliefs I am considering here can be expected to change and can be expected to change not only through the agency of lived experience, but through the experience of entertaining fictions as well.

3. M. H. Abrams, ed., Foreword to *Literature and Belief*, English Institute Essays, 1957 (New York: Columbia University Press, 1958), p. viii. It is interesting that Abrams says it is no longer belief in the first kind of assertion that we worry about, but only belief in the second kind. Perhaps the *worry* is gone, but certainly the theoretical interest is still very much there. But in any case, these two kinds of literary belief are closely related, for our willingness to go along with either sort depends very much upon our willingness to go along with the other.

4. I should emphasize that the oscillation I am imagining here is not between belief and disbelief; I am not endorsing the theory that in entertaining fictions we move rapidly between belief and disbelief, and I am continuing to

argue that readers simultaneously believe and disbelieve. The oscillation I have in mind is between states of absorption at one extreme of which beliefs in the fiction seem weakly held and disbeliefs are particularly evident, while at the other extreme, beliefs are particularly evident and disbeliefs seem weak.

5. For some purposes, probability was seen by the Augustans as mediating between truth and fiction, but at the same time its Aristotelian and neoclassical association with universals and reason put it clearly on the side of truth. See Patey, *Probability and Literary Form,* pp. 140–141 for a discussion of this instability.

6. Inner consistency has often been taken to be an important criterion of fictional probability, and some writers go so far as to equate probability and consistency, although Patey in *Probability and Literary Form* shows why this is mistaken (pp. 142–143 and 163). If probability *were* equated with inner consistency, might not the formula avoid my antinomy? That is, if probability were simply a matter of relations between propositions in a fictional text, then could we not imagine a perfectly reasonable ascription of probability to various statements we might make about elements of that text? We could indeed, but only if the fiction made no reference to anything in the real world and bore no relationship with anything in the real world. Thus we could invent a purely abstract possible world and, following its givens, we could judge the probability of events imagined within it. Such would indeed be a fictional world that never raised for us my antinomy. But no literary fictional world is like this. All literary fictional worlds, even the most fantastic, are clearly founded upon the real world and refer to the real world (invite us to compare them with the real world) in a host of ways.

Conclusion
Probability, Play, and the Novel

1. See esp. chap. 1, "Realism and the Novel Form," in Watt, *Rise of the Novel,* pp. 9–34. Michael McKeon's new and formidable *The Origins of the English Novel, 1600–1740* (Baltimore: Johns Hopkins University Press, 1987) seems a likely contender to displace Watt's account. McKeon, however, does not seem to regard probability as an especially problematic or central concept.

2. One of the best recent accounts of the origins of the novel is Walter Reed's in *An Exemplary History of the Novel: The Quixotic versus the Picaresque*

(Chicago: University of Chicago Press, 1981); like McKeon, Reed usefully widens Watt's nationalistic and theoretical horizons.

3. Watt, *Rise of the Novel*, p. 32.

4. Ibid.

5. Ibid., pp. 10–11. See also for useful accounts of the history and meaning of *realism*, Richard Stang, *The Theory of the Novel in England: 1850–1870* (New York: Columbia University Press, 1959), pp. 148–149 and Raymond Williams, *Keywords: A Vocabulary of Culture and Society* (New York: Oxford University Press, 1976), pp. 216–221.

6. Of course, as we have already noted, there is no shortage of first-rate critics happy to take realism seriously and at the same time perfectly alert to the theoretical problems that attend realism. In addition to the books by Romano, Arac, Caserio, and Ermarth previously noted (chap. 5, n. 21), we should also note George Levine's *The Realistic Imagination: English Fiction from Frankenstein to Lady Chatterly* (Chicago: University of Chicago Press, 1981), whose first chapter provides an excellent summary of the theoretical vicissitudes of realism.

7. Watt, *Rise of the Novel*, p. 33.

8. Nelson, *Fact or Fiction* (cited chap. 4, n. 20) and Lennard Davis, *Factual Fictions: The Origins of the English Novel* (New York: Columbia University Press, 1983). McKeon's *Origins of the English Novel* is also centrally concerned with the evolution of the fact/fictions distinction.

9. Nelson, *Fact or Fiction*, pp. 36–37 and see also Herschel Baker, *The Race of Time* (Toronto: University of Toronto Press, 1967), pp. 35ff.

10. "Daniel Defoe: Lies as Truth," in Davis, *Factual Fictions*, pp. 154–173.

11. Herbert Spencer, *The Principles of Psychology* (1855; reprint, New York: D. Appleton and Co. 1890).

12. Karl Groos, *The Play of Animals* (1896; reprint, New York: Arno Press, 1976) and *The Play of Man* (1900; reprint, New York: Arno Press, 1976).

13. Sigmund Freud, *Beyond the Pleasure Principle,* trans. James Strachey (1920; reprint, New York: Liveright, 1950).

14. Erik Erikson, *Play and Development* (New York: W. W. Norton and Co., 1972) and D. W. Winnicott, *Playing and Reality* (London: Tavistock Publications, 1971).

15. Jean Piaget, *Play, Dreams, and Imitation in Childhood,* trans. C. Gattegno and F. M. Hodgson (1951; reprint, London: Routledge and Kegan Paul, 1962).

16. Johan Huizinga, *Homo Ludens* (New York: Roy Publishers, 1950), p. 173.

17. Ibid., p. 205.

18. Ibid., p. 18.

19. Ibid., p. 28.

20. Jacques Derrida, "Structure, Sign, and Play in the Discourse of the Human Sciences," in *Writing and Difference* (Chicago: University of Chicago Press, 1978), p. 292. This essay is in fact a plausible place to begin.

21. As quoted by Culler, *On Deconstruction*, pp. 165–166. A different translation appears in Jacques Derrida, *Positions*, trans. Alan Bass (Chicago: University of Chicago Press, 1972), p. 41.

22. Jacques Derrida, *Of Grammatology*, trans. Gayatri Chakravorty Spivack (Baltimore: Johns Hopkins University Press, 1976), p. 159.

23. The controversial questions are raised by Frank Lentricchia in "History or the Abyss: Poststructuralism," in *After the New Criticism* (Chicago: University of Chicago Press, 1980), pp. 156–210.

24. Virginia Woolf, *The Common Reader*, New Edition (London: Hogarth Press, 1933), p. 213.

25. Philippe Ariès, *Centuries of Childhood*, trans. Robert Baldick (New York: Alfred A. Knopf, 1962).

26. Ibid., pp. 68–71.

27. Ibid., p. 71.

28. See for example Arbuthnot, "An Argument" (cited chap. 5, n. 15), which is discussed both by Hacking, *Emergence of Probability*, pp. 166–171 and by Patey, *Probability and Literary Form*, pp. 70–72, 73.

29. Toulmin, *Uses of Argument*, p. 85.

30. It is significant that Toulmin argues for the reality or seriousness of the assertions probabilists make, but at the same time argues that "probability" itself does not exist. Recall his claim that "the abstract noun 'probability'—despite what we learnt at our kindergartens about nouns being words that stand for things—not merely has no tangible counterpart, referent, *designatum* or what you will, not merely does not name a thing of whatever kind, but is a word of such a type that it is nonsense even to talk about it as denoting, standing for, or naming anything" (Ibid.).

31. For our purposes, a perhaps even better debate about the evidence of books versus that of things occurs in chap. 11 of Charlotte Lennox, *The Female Quixote, or the Adventures of Arabella.*

32. See Patey's appendix C *(Probability and Literary Form)*, tabulating "the vocabulary of conjecture and expectation in *Emma*," p. 281.

33. Gregory Bateson, "A Theory of Play and Fantasy," *Psychiatric Research Reports* 2 (1955): 39–51, reprinted in J. S. Bruner, A. Jolly, and K. Sylva, eds.,

Play: Its Role in Development and Evolution (Harmondsworth: Penguin, 1976), p. 120.

34. Piaget also distinguishes a third sort of play, games with rules. The three types of play are significant for him because they correspond with the three stages in the development of the child's intelligence.

35. Bateson, "Theory of Play," p. 121.

36. Ibid.

37. Douglas Hofstadter, *Gödel, Escher, Bach: An Eternal Golden Braid* (New York: Basic Books, 1979).

38. Tzvetan Todorov, "Introduction," *Communications,* 11 (1968): 2, my translation. This essay is reprinted in the collection of Todorov's essays *La Poétique de la Prose,* which has been translated by Richard Howard under the title *The Poetics of Prose* (Ithaca: Cornell University Press, 1977), pp. 80–88.

Index